Bush v. Gore

Bush v. Gore

Controversial Presidential Election Case

Diana K. Sergis

Landmark Supreme Court Cases

Enslow Publishers, Inc.

40 Industrial Road   PO Box 38
Box 398   Aldershot
Berkeley Heights, NJ 07922   Hants GU12 6BP
USA   UK

http://www.enslow.com

Library of Congress Cataloguing-in-Publication Data

Sergis, Diana K.
    Bush v. Gore : controversial presidential election case / Diana K. Sergis.
        v. cm. — (Landmark Supreme Court cases)
    Includes bibliographical references and index.
    Contents: Building a case — Electing a president as set by the
constitution — The road to the Supreme Court — The case for George W.
Bush — The case for Al Gore — The decision — Where do we stand today?
    ISBN 0-7660-2095-9 (hardcover)
    1. Bush, George W. (George Walker), 1946—Trials, litigation,
etc.—Juvenile literature. 2. Gore, Albert, 1948—Trials, litigation,
etc.—Juvenile literature. 3. United States. Supreme Court—Juvenile
literature. 4. Presidents—United States—Election—2000—Juvenile
literature. 5. Contested elections—United States—Juvenile literature.
6. Bush, George W. (George Walker), 1946—Trials, litigation, etc. [1.
Gore, Albert, 1948—Trials, litigation, etc. 2. United States. Supreme
Court. 3. Presidents—United States—Election—2000. 4. Contested
elections.] I. Title: Bush versus Gore. II. Title. III. Series.
KF5074.2.S47 2003
342.73'075—dc21

                                                    2002154646

Printed in the United States of America

10 9 8 7 6 5 4 3 2 1

To Our Readers: We have done our best to make sure that all Internet addresses in this book
were active and appropriate when we went to press. However, the author and publisher have
no control over and assume no liability for the material available on those Internet sites or on
other Web sites they may link to. Any comments or suggestions can be sent by e-mail to
comments@enslow.com or to the address on the back cover.

Photo Credits: © Corel Corporation, pp. 9, 52, 60, 103; Andy Nelson/©1999
The Christian Science Monitor, pp. 13, 14, 66; Associated Press, pp. 96, 107;
Bennett/©2000 The Christian Science Monitor, p. 89; Dover Publications, Inc., p.
32; Enslow Publishers, Inc., pp. 10, 20; George Bush Presidential Library, p. 41;
John Bavaro, p. 26; Lannis Waters/Palm Beach Post, p. 23; Library of Congress, pp.
34, 37, 38, 87; Photos.com, p. 109; Richard Graulich/Palm Beach Post, p. 22;
Scott Wiseman/Palm Beach Post, pp. 47, 49, 76; Sgt. Lou Briscese, USAF, p. 91;
Supreme Court Historical Society, United States Supreme Court, Washington,
D.C., pp. 62, 69, 83; The Supreme Court of the United States Office of the
Curator, p. 81.

Cover Illustration: Bennett/©2000 The Christian Science Monitor

Contents

Dedication

For Elaine, Lee, and David

I am indebted to my family and close friends for their constant support and encouragement; and most especially to my sisters, Carol Sergis and Nancy Pappas, and my "brother," Peter Pappas, for their critique of the manuscript—from start to finish.

"An accurate vote count is one of the essential foundations of our democracy." —Chief Justice Charles Wells, Florida Supreme Court, *Bush* v. *Palm Beach Canvassing Board*, November 21, 2000.

"The counting of votes that are of questionable legality does in my view threaten irreparable harm . . . to the country." —Justice Antonin Scalia, United States Supreme Court, concurring opinion to the Court's order to stop the hand recounts in Florida, December 9, 2000.

Introduction

Something extraordinary happened during the presidential election of 2000. For one thing, the winner was not known until December 12. That was thirty-five days after the November 7 election. (Most of the votes are counted on Election Day. So, the winner is usually announced that same night.) But more importantly, the voters did not make the final decision in this election. Neither did Congress. Quite surprisingly, the United States Supreme Court did. Its ruling, in effect, decided who would be the new forty-third president of the United States. The highest court in the land had never before made such a decision in the history of the nation. What went wrong? What went right?

Over 105 million Americans cast their votes for president on Election Day, 2000. Then, a rather routine race suddenly took an unusual turn. Neither of the two leading candidates could declare victory. They were Vice President

Albert Gore (a Democrat) and Texas Governor George W. Bush (a Republican). Gore had the most popular votes in the nation's total. But neither Gore nor Bush had enough electoral votes to win.

Doesn't the candidate with the most popular votes automatically win? No, to win a presidential election, a candidate must get at least 270 (out of 538) electoral votes. Electoral votes and popular votes are not the same. Voters go to the polling booths to cast their "popular" ballots in a presidential election. That means they do not vote directly for a president. Instead, they vote for "electors" who will, in turn, vote for their candidate for president. These electors make up a body known as the Electoral College. Is this a fair system? This question has been debated ever since the founding fathers set up this system in the Constitution.

In modern times, the president has usually won both the popular votes and the electoral votes. However, the immediate results of the 2000 election presented a rare but serious problem. As of November 8, 2000, Gore had over half a million popular votes more than Bush nationwide. Gore had 260 electoral votes to Bush's 246 electoral votes. The outcome of the presidential election finally hinged on who would win the twenty-five electoral votes in the state of Florida. But determining the winner was not as simple as it might seem. The process was bogged down in the counting of Florida's nearly 6 million popular votes.

Bush won the popular votes in Florida—twice.

The outcome of the presidential election in 2000 depended on which candidate won the electoral votes in the state of Florida.

Officials, by law, had to repeat the machine recount because Bush's first lead was too slim. Then Gore (as was his legal right) asked for a hand recount of some ballots. He believed the machine counts of these ballots were not accurate. Bush sued to stop these hand recounts. He believed that the process of counting punch-card ballots by hand was not legal because it lacked standards. Then, Gore sued to continue these hand recounts. Was either one just a sore loser, or were they both right to contest the vote counts?

Time (or the lack of it) played an extremely important role in the outcome of this election. Which deadlines were questionable, and which could not be changed? One court ruling was challenged by yet another court case. So, the legal battles in Florida dragged on and on. Gore wanted to "count every vote" in Florida. But how many times was enough? That was Bush's argument.

Was there enough time to recount by hand all the Florida votes (or even just the contested ones)? Then, too, there were no clear standards for counting ballots by hand statewide. So how fair was any recount result? The United States Supreme Court questioned these two sticky points. For this and other reasons, the Court felt it had to grant Bush's requests to sort out the legal wrangling that prolonged the election deadlock. But keep in mind that the country had a sitting president (President Bill Clinton) who

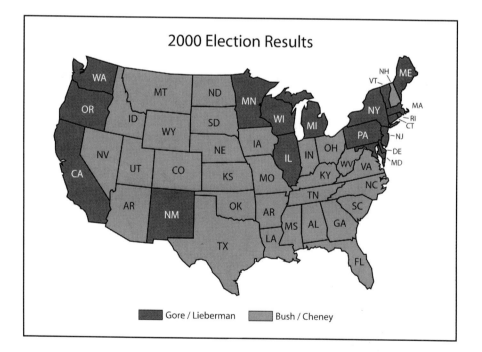

2000 Election Results

Gore / Lieberman   Bush / Cheney

would serve through this period until the morning of January 20, 2001, when the new president-elect would be sworn in. So, was the sense of urgency real, or simply fueled by politics and news reporters?

The United States Supreme Court made a landmark decision in the *Bush* v. *Gore* case. So, it remains a one-of-a-kind case. Or does it? Will the high court step into a presidential election deadlock in the future? Will voters who felt they were bypassed in the 2000 election trust in the legal system the next time around? Only time will tell.

The Court's decision also left many other unanswered questions. Was the Court's action too hasty? Did it sidestep the election process set in place by the framers of the Constitution? Which candidate would Congress have chosen if it were allowed to decide? Who would really have won in Florida if *all* the ballots were recounted by hand? Read on to find out some of the answers—the ones that are based on fact. For other answers, which are based on opinion, you will need to decide for yourself.

1

Building a Case

Election Day is usually filled with promise. But it spelled trouble on November 7, 2000. It turned out to be the beginning of a roller-coaster ride for Vice President Al Gore, who served under President Clinton, 1993–2000, and Texas Governor George W. Bush. These two leading presidential candidates had campaigned long and hard.

Bush's seventeen-month presidential campaign cost over $185 million. He billed himself as a "uniter, not a divider," and promised to work with Congress to get things done.[1] (The Clinton White House was often at odds with Congress.) Bush's three main campaign promises were excellent schools, tax relief, and a strong military. When he won the nomination of the Republican Party, Bush chose Dick Cheney as his running mate for vice president. Cheney had served as secretary of defense for a former president—George Herbert Walker Bush, George W. Bush's father.

Gore's campaign cost more than $120 million. He focused on three main issues: the economy, education, and health care. Though the economy was in great shape at that time, Gore refused to run on President Clinton's coattails. (Some experts say this mistake, coupled with a poorly run campaign, may have cost him the White House.) Gore chose Senator Joseph Lieberman as his Democratic running mate. Lieberman was a United States senator from

George W. Bush promised to focus on schooling, tax relief, and a strong military if he were to be elected president.

Al Gore promised to focus on strengthening the economy, the education system, and health care if he were to be elected president.

Connecticut. He was the first Jewish candidate to run in a presidential race.

The candidates voted early and went home to wait for the results. Governor Bush waited at the governor's mansion in Austin, Texas. Vice President Gore waited in Nashville, Tennessee, his home state. But now it was time for the voters to speak. Some political experts thought it would be a close race. But no one expected this race to be so out of the ordinary that it would be studied later in history and law books.

Election Night Results: November 7, 2000

Voters cast more than 105 million ballots on Election Day, 2000. Al Gore led George W. Bush by about 539,897 popular votes nationwide. He had 255 electoral votes. Bush had 246 electoral votes. Each man waited to reach the necessary total of 270 electoral votes to become the new president.

Television stations quickly reported election night results, state by state. Finally, it was down to three states: Florida (with twenty-five electoral votes), Oregon (with seven electoral votes), and New Mexico (with five electoral votes). Attention quickly turned to Florida. Its twenty-five electoral votes would put either man over the top.

Gore eventually won in New Mexico and lost in Oregon. In all, he won in twenty states and the District of Columbia, with a total of 267 electoral votes. Bush won twenty-nine states, with 246 electoral votes.

Most of the polls closed in Florida at 7 P.M. The television networks raced to be the first to report the election results there. About an hour later, they projected Al Gore as the winner in that state. At 9:30 P.M., Bush's representatives called the networks and told them their sources showed that he was slightly ahead. They correctly predicted that it was going to be "a long night."[2]

Indeed, Election Night never seemed to end. The television news networks made one slipup after another. Shortly before 10 P.M., they pulled Florida back from the Gore "win" column. By 1 A.M., Bush was leading in that state by 200,000 popular votes. The networks declared Bush the winner in Florida around 2:30 A.M.

Gore called Bush half an hour later to tell the governor he was bowing out of the race. Then, he prepared a speech to admit defeat to the public. But a curious thing happened next. A Gore aide checked election results on a Florida Web site. It showed new vote totals as precincts counted and then reported them. The aide spotted Bush's lead slipping and told Gore. The vice president decided to cancel his speech. He phoned Bush back at around 3:45 A.M. to take back his concession. No presidential candidate had ever done this before.

"As you may have noticed," Gore told Bush, "things have changed."

"Well, you need to do what you ... need to do," Bush responded.

"Well, there's no reason to get snippy," Gore shot back. Bush slammed the phone down.[3] Understandably, Bush was upset by Gore's sudden turnabout—he and his family had no clue that their victory would last for only forty-five minutes.

After Gore's second phone call, the television networks flip-flopped once again. The Florida election returns now

16

showed that Bush's lead was too slim. So, the networks were forced to take Florida back from the Bush "win" column.

What was going on? The networks all used the same source for election returns—the Voter News Service (VNS). As it turned out, this service had based its findings on incorrect samplings of exit polls, and not actual returns. (Exit polls are surveys typically taken of how people voted in key political districts.)

Tom Brokaw, a television news anchor, summed up the networks' embarrassment over their clumsy news coverage. "We don't have egg on our face," he said. "We have an omelet."[4] Indeed, the networks wiped egg off their faces for days.

The First Florida Recount

Now all eyes were on Florida, the third most populous state in the nation. More than 6 million Florida voters had cast their ballots for president on November 7, 2000. The next day, Bush officially led by 1,784 popular votes. (He had received 2,909,135 votes to Gore's 2,907,351 votes. Other candidates had received a total of 139,616 votes.) But the results did not mean that Bush was the official winner in Florida, and as a result, the newly elected president. Bush's lead was less than "one half of a percent . . . of the votes cast."[5] Florida law required an automatic machine recount of ballots in close races such as this one.

The results of the automatic machine recount showed

that Bush's lead in Florida shrunk to nearly 300 popular votes. But this recount produced questionable results. A curious detail was later reported. Eighteen counties failed to run the ballots through the counting machines a second time. Instead, election supervisors checked the records of the machine totals taken on the day of the election. This meant that 1.25 million votes were not recounted.[6]

In addition, the machines still rejected overvotes and undervotes on punch-card ballots, as they had the first time around. "Overvotes" were ballots that voters punched more than once. "Undervotes" were ballots for which no votes were recorded. One reason for this was that voters simply might not have voted for president. More likely, the machines could not count these ballots due to hanging chads, or the small pieces left over from the punched paper holes on the ballots. If the chads were not completely punched clear of the holes, they were left hanging. Florida officials estimated that there were more than 62,000 undervotes statewide.

Were there any solutions to these problems? Bush claimed that both overvotes and undervotes were not actual votes. He argued, therefore, that there was no need to further recount these ballots. Gore claimed that undervotes were actual votes that the machines missed. He argued that the machines were at fault, and not the voters. He wanted election officials to review each ballot and decide the voter's intent. Also, people who said they voted twice by mistake (overvoting) wanted to vote anew.

On November 9, Al Gore officially asked for the votes to be recounted by hand. Because Florida law did not provide for hand recounts statewide, Gore would have to request a hand recount county by county. His strategy was to zero in on four select counties: Volusia, Palm Beach, Broward, and Miami-Dade. These were the counties where he believed the types of voting machines or the ballots themselves (punch cards) were faulty. These counties were also heavily Democratic, so Gore expected quick gains.

Florida's Troublesome Ballots

There are different methods of voting and different types of voting equipment nationwide. People vote by machine, hand ballots, overseas military ballots, or absentee ballots, which they mail in. Oregon was the only state to use mail-in ballots exclusively in the 2000 election.

In the 2000 election, four ballot systems were used throughout Florida's sixty-seven counties. These included optical scanners, punch cards, levers, and paper. Forty-one counties used optical scanners. Here, voters used pencils to mark the boxes on the paper ballots. They placed the ballots in a machine. A computer scanned the darkest marks and added up the totals. If voters made errors, they could ask for new ballots. Twenty-four counties used punch cards. Here, voters punched the holes opposite the candidate's name. Computers read the punch cards. Only one county used the lever machine. Here, voters pushed the handle down next to

County	Bush/ Cheney	Gore/ Lieberman	County	Bush/ Cheney	Gore/ Lieberman
Alachua	11	15	Leon	11	17
Baker	1	0	Levy	5	0
Bay	45	23	Liberty	0	0
Bradford	2	0	Madison	0	1
Brevard	68	23	Manatee	71	49
Broward	37	57	Marion	5	9
Calhoun	0	1	Martin	2	1
Charlotte	2	1	Miami-Dade	41	59
Citrus	34	6	Monroe	4	4
Clay	167	36	Nassau	4	3
Collier	17	18	Okaloosa	93	41
Columbia	4	2	Okeechobee	0	1
Desoto	0	1	Orange	14	16
Dixie	0	1	Osceola	25	6
Duval	362	175	Palm Beach	13	22
Escambia	154	47	Pasco	25	12
Flagler	5	0	Pinellas	24	27
Franklin	0	1	Polk	15	7
Gadsden	3	1	Putnam	10	5
Gilchrist	0	0	Santa Rosa	65	16
Glades	0	0	Sarasota	17	16
Gulf	3	1	Seminole	113	53
Hamilton	1	1	St. Johns	18	7
Hardee	0	3	St. Lucie	0	1
Hendry	0	0	Sumter	0	0
Hernando	12	4	Suwannee	3	1
Highlands	1	2	Taylor	2	0
Hillsborough	34	19	Union	0	0
Holmes	1	0	Volusia	11	9
Indian River	4	1	Wakulla	0	0
Jackson	1	2	Walton	4	1
Jefferson	0	0	Washington	1	0
Lafayette	0	0			
Lake	0	0	**Total**	1,575	836
Lee	10	11	**Percent**	63.3%	33.6%

Florida votes by county.

the candidate's name. Machines tracked the totals. Only one county used the paper system. Here, voters used pencils to mark the boxes on paper ballots. They dropped the ballots in a box. Officials gathered and counted these paper ballots. Machines then totaled them up.

Although no voting system is foolproof, the punch-card system, in particular, had built-in problems. If voters did not punch the holes cleanly through, the machines could not "read" their votes. Some people argued that clearly stated instructions were posted for the voters. Yet, did most voters read the instructions?

AFTER VOTING, CHECK YOUR BALLOT CARD TO BE SURE YOUR VOTING SELECTIONS ARE CLEARLY AND CLEANLY PUNCHED, AND THERE ARE NO CHIPS LEFT HANGING ON THE BACK OF THE CARD.[7]

The "Butterfly" Ballot

More than 6,000 voters in Palm Beach County complained about the "butterfly" ballot. It was a new style of punch card designed by Theresa LePore. She was the County Elections Supervisor of Palm Beach. Oddly enough, LePore said she designed the butterfly ballot for easy use. She used large

Some votes were not counted because the chad, shown here on a fingertip, was left hanging on the ballot. When this happened, the machine that counted the votes was not able to read the ballot.

print for the candidates' names to make the ballot easier for senior citizens to read. But the large print took up extra space, so the names were placed differently from the way voters were used to seeing them. The names of Al Gore and Pat Buchanan, the Reform Party candidate, faced each other on opposite pages. The punch holes lined up down the middle of the facing pages.

Many voters claimed they meant to vote for Al Gore. But they were confused by the layout of the ballot. They said they marked their ballots twice—once by mistake for

Pat Buchanan, and then once again for Gore. Voting twice only served to cancel their "overvotes."

Legal arguments over ballot recounts would become hurdles in a race against time. Thirty-six days passed before the outcome of the 2000 election was finally decided. But the delay was not so unique, for this election had its roots in American history. So, too, did many of the solutions to the deadlock problems.

Theresa LePore, left, designed the butterfly ballot for easy use. However, many voters found the new ballots difficult to understand. Judge Charles E. Burton, right, worked with many others to read questionable ballots such as this one during the hand recounts.

2

Electing a President as Set by the Constitution

The 2000 presidential election now serves as an important history lesson in American government and politics. As the people watched the unusual events unfold on television, they witnessed history in the making. They also had a first-hand look at the actual process of electing a president. How many viewers knew how the Electoral College worked before this—or had even heard of it?

The actions of the United States Supreme Court in the *Bush* v. *Gore* case took many people by surprise. Is this the branch of government that is supposed to decide the winner in a close presidential election?

Questions like these underscored the need for many Americans to get to know how their government works.

Most of the answers are spelled out in the United States Constitution.

Shared Powers

The United States Constitution is a remarkable document. Its framers included James Madison, Alexander Hamilton, and Benjamin Franklin. The Constitution provides a framework for the structure and management of a strong national government. Although it was ratified in 1788, the Constitution still works for modern times. How? There are many key factors. One is its built-in system of checks and balances among the different branches of government.

The Constitution sets up three branches of federal government: legislative, executive, and judicial. Each branch functions separately and independently. The legislative branch, or Congress, makes the law. The executive branch, which includes the office of the president, carries out the law. The judicial branch is the federal court system that includes the United States Supreme Court. Overall, these courts are responsible for protecting the rights of the individual as they relate to the rules of law. To carry out this task, courts must interpret the meaning of the law.

All three branches also share power and responsibilities. Together, they provide a system of checks and balances. In this way, each branch of government is held accountable. How does this system of checks and balances work? Take, for example, the judicial branch. It has the power to review and overturn the rulings of the lower courts and the actions taken by the executive branch. It can also review and overturn laws passed by Congress (federal lawmakers) and by state lawmakers.

How did the system of checks and balances operate in the Bush v. Gore case?

The United States Supreme Court usually respects a state court's ruling on a legal issue related to its own state's constitution.[1] But in this case, the Court decided on what it

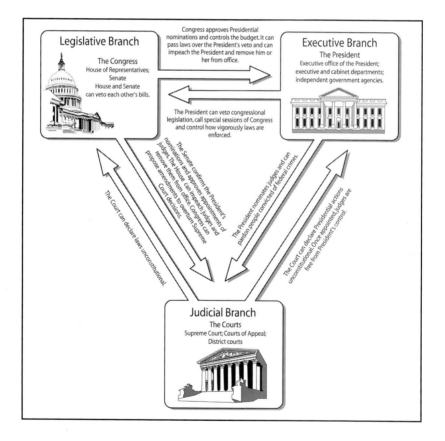

believed was a state supreme court's questionable rulings in the 2000 presidential election vote battles. The Court's focus was on whether the state court wrongfully stepped on the powers granted to the state lawmakers and election officials. Did the Florida Supreme Court interpret the law or make a new law? Or did the United States Supreme Court overstep its bounds by taking the case? (See Chapter 6.)

The Constitution also provides for the sharing of powers between state governments and the national government. Then, too, there are powers granted only to the states, such as the running of elections. Generally, the states leave this responsibility to the counties.

The Electoral College

In the 2000 election, Gore received more than 48 percent of the popular vote nationwide. That meant he received more than half a million popular votes more than George W. Bush. However, Bush eventually won a majority of the electoral votes nationwide. He had 271 electoral votes to Gore's 267 electoral votes. Why did George W. Bush win the presidency over Al Gore? Again, the answer can be found in the Constitution.

The framers of the Constitution did not want the people to vote directly for the president. Why? They were afraid of the abuse of power by one or more persons. For example, a dictator might sway the public (who were, at that time, largely uneducated) and take control of the nation. Or, a mob might seize power. To safeguard against such possibilities, the framers established the Electoral College system.

The Electoral College is not a college in the typical sense; it is not a school or university. It is a body of 538 members, who are called "electors." The electors—not the entire voting public—vote directly for the president and the vice president. After the popular election, the winning slate of electors in each state casts its state's total of "electoral" votes. A candidate for president needs a minimum of 270 out of a total of 538 electoral votes to win. That is a simple majority, or one vote over half of the total.

Does each state have the same number of electors? No, the Constitution provides a means to determine each state's total of electors. It says that each state names electors equal to the number of its senators (always two) and its representatives in Congress. The number of representatives in a given state depends on its population. But over the years, a state's population can go up, down, or stay the same. So, a national census, or poll, is taken every ten years to count the number of people who live in each state.

In this system, the states with higher populations have more electors than less populated states. For example, California, which has the highest population in the nation, has thirty-two electoral votes. Alaska, a state with one of the lowest populations, has three electoral votes. The District of Columbia, the seat of the national government, has three electors. (The Twenty-third Amendment to the Constitution gave this right to Washington, D.C., in 1961.)

Selection of Presidential Electors

How are presidential electors chosen? Article II of the Constitution says that state lawmakers can make this decision. In the United States Supreme Court's majority decision in the *Bush* v. *Gore* case, the Justices were careful to remind us of that. "The individual citizen has no federal constitutional right to vote for electors for the President of the United States," the Supreme Court said, "unless and until the state [lawmakers choose] a statewide election" to do so.[2]

That means each state has its own election laws. It also means each state (and the District of Columbia) selects its own electors. In the early days, the lawmakers in all the states chose them. Today, the voters in some states pick them. But in most states, each major political party usually names its own slate of electors.

What is a slate of electors? In each state, the political parties draw up individual lists of potential electors for their candidate. Which slate of electors in a state gets to actually vote? A slate of electors becomes the state's electors when their candidate wins the state's popular votes. (The voting public determines the "popular" vote count for the state. In most states, the names of the electors are not even listed on the popular ballots.) What happens if there is a problem about which slate is the official slate of a state? That state is supposed to try to solve it.

The Role of Presidential Electors

The members of the Electoral College meet every four years. They do not, however, meet as an entire group. Actually, the winning slate of electors in each state meets in its own state capital in mid-December. There, the electors cast their votes for president and vice president. (The voting public has already cast popular votes on Election Day in early November.)

Typically, a slate of electors pledges to vote for its candidate who won the popular vote in their state. Forty-eight states have this winner-takes-all policy. That means the presidential candidate who wins the state's popular votes also gets all the state's electoral votes. The two exceptions are Maine (with four electoral votes) and Nebraska (with five electoral votes). In these states, only two of its electors are chosen based on the candidate who won the statewide popular vote. The popular vote winner in each of their House districts determines the other electors.

However, like Al Gore, the winner of the national popular vote may not always win the majority of electoral votes. This can happen in very close races between two candidates. It can also happen in races including several third-party candidates. Then, one candidate may not receive the necessary 270 electoral votes.

30

Basically, the nation has a two-party political system— the Democratic Party and the Republican Party. Third parties play important roles, too. For example, they may offer new or different ideas. Or, they may challenge the policies of the other political parties.

How did third-party candidates affect the 2000 election? There were several third-party candidates in that presidential race. Two third-party candidates of note were Ralph Nader and Pat Buchanan. Nader ran as a candidate of the Green Party. He was considered the "spoiler" because he drew votes away from Gore. He received about 3 percent of the popular votes nationwide. Buchanan ran as a candidate of the Reform Party. He received less than one percent of the national popular vote. But some experts claimed he received more than his share of intended votes in Palm Beach, Florida. They said that was because of the county's confusing butterfly ballots.

What happens if two candidates are tied in electoral votes? In this event, the Constitution provides a solution. That is, the members of the House of Representatives vote by secret ballot. But each state's group of Representatives to the House is allowed only one vote.

Why didn't Congress step in to elect a president when Bush and Gore were deadlocked? Remember, in the 2000 presidential election, Bush and Gore did not have a tie in the electoral vote count. Rather, these two candidates contested Florida's popular vote totals in the courts.

Electoral Deadlocks of the Past

George W. Bush was not the only presidential candidate who lacked a majority of the electoral votes but who went on to win the presidency. There were others, from as early as 1800. The first two presidential elections ran smoothly enough. In fact, George Washington, the first president, was elected unanimously. But it was not too long before problems arose that the framers of the Constitution did not foresee—electoral deadlocks. Three historic elections of the 1800s resulted in electoral problems.

Election of 1800: An electoral deadlock has happened twice in American history. The first time was during the election of 1800. At that time, the Constitution called for

the person with the most electoral votes to be chosen president. The candidate with the second highest total of electoral votes would be elected the vice president. In 1800, Thomas Jefferson and Aaron Burr were tied for president. The election was thrown into the hands of Congress, which voted for Jefferson.

Thomas Jefferson

32

In response to the election deadlock of 1800, the Twelfth Amendment was made into law four years later. This amendment changed the electoral voting system with its several requirements. It says electors must vote for president and vice president separately. The winning candidate for each office must receive a majority of the electoral votes. Otherwise, Congress decides the election outcome. In that event, the House of Representatives chooses the president. The Senate chooses the vice president.

The Twelfth Amendment also says that the president and vice president cannot reside in the same state. (Lawmakers wanted to avoid favoritism by electors who might otherwise vote only for candidates from their home states.) On December 1, 2000, some Democratic voters in Texas used this amendment to challenge George W. Bush in court. The case was called *Jones* v. *Bush*.[3]

They claimed that George W. Bush and his running mate, Dick Cheney, were both residents of Texas. Cheney was a former congressional representative from Wyoming. He moved to Texas in 1993. But on July 21, 2000, he reregistered to vote in Jackson Hole, Wyoming, where he has a house. That was four days before Bush officially picked him as his vice-presidential running mate. An appeals court decided the case on December 7, 2000. It ruled that Cheney's primary home was in Wyoming. (An appeals court reviews a lower court's ruling on a case at the request of one of the parties in a lawsuit.)

This political cartoon depicts the presidential race between Andrew Jackson and John Quincy Adams.

Election of 1824: The second electoral deadlock occurred during the election of 1824. None of the candidates received a majority of electoral votes, even though Andrew Jackson led in popular votes. The election was thrown into the House of Representatives. The House decided on John Quincy Adams over the three other candidates.

John Quincy Adams has two interesting footnotes in history. One is that he and Thomas Jefferson were the only two presidents ever elected by the House of Representatives. The other is that his father, John Adams, was a former president (1797–1801). They were the first pair of father-son presidents. Who is the only other pair of father-son presidents? It is George Herbert Bush (1989–1993) and his son, George Walker Bush (2001–).

Election of 1876: The election of 1876 also resulted in a rather unusual electoral deadlock. Rutherford B. Hayes, the Republican candidate, ran against Samuel J. Tilden, the Democratic candidate. Tilden won the popular vote. But there was confusion about the electoral vote totals. Four states sent double sets of electoral votes to Congress. With each pair, one set was for Tilden while the other was for Hayes.

The Constitution did not provide a way to handle this type of problem. But this time Congress did not pass an amendment. Instead, it created the special Electoral Commission in 1877 to decide who would be the new president. The commission was made up of fourteen members from both houses of Congress and from the Supreme Court. When the members finally reached a compromise, Hayes was voted in as the new president.

Constitutional Amendments and Presidential Transfer of Power

In addition to the Twelfth Amendment, lawmakers still felt that more guidelines were needed for a smoother transfer of power from one president to the next. Two amendments to the Constitution were passed to deal with this issue. One (the Twentieth Amendment) dealt with transfer of power should anything happen to a president-elect or a vice president-elect. (A president-elect or a vice president-elect has been elected but has not been sworn into office yet.) The other (the Twenty-fifth Amendment) dealt with transfer of power should anything happen to a president who is already in office. A third amendment (the Twenty-second Amendment) dealt with the possibility that a popular president may have too much power if he or she stayed in office too long. These three amendments are explained below.

Twentieth Amendment: It came into law in 1933. It gives guidelines in the event that the president-elect or the vice president-elect dies or is disqualified. It says that the vice president-elect steps into the first position unless or until a president is finally chosen.

This amendment also set January 20 as the new date when the terms of the president and vice president end. Previously, that date was March 4. The change also shortens the period of time during which the new Congress meets. That means the defeated senators and representatives have a shorter time in office before the new Congress and the new president and vice president take office.

Twenty-fifth Amendment: What happens if a president or vice president becomes too ill, dies, resigns, or is removed from office? (After all, eight presidents have died in office, and one president has resigned.) Congress passed the Twenty-fifth Amendment in 1967. It provides for a smoother transfer of power for either office.

Then, as now, if there is no sitting president, the vice president takes over as president. But now if a sitting president is too ill to fulfill the duties of the office, the vice

One of the strengths of the Constitution of the United States is that changes, or amendments, can be made to the document. Ever since the first ten amendments—called the Bill of Rights—were adopted in 1791, changes have been made to the Constitution to clarify the role of the government, establish the rights of the people, and address the changing needs of the country.

president takes over as acting president. Also, if anything happens to a sitting vice president, the president chooses a new vice president. But both houses of Congress must confirm the selection. (In the past, a vacancy in the office of vice president was not filled until the next election.)

What if the offices of the presidency and vice presidency are both vacant? The order of presidential succession has changed over time. First, a 1792 law required a new election. Next, an 1886 law said the secretary of state became the president. Then, a 1947 law said the speaker of the House of Representatives became president. This law is still in effect.

Twenty-second Amendment: Can a president be re-elected again and again? At one time, it was a possibility. However, presidents (from John Adams to Calvin Coolidge) followed the two-term (eight-year) tradition started by George Washington. Then along came Franklin Roosevelt. He was first elected in 1932, and then

The first president of the United States, George Washington, started the tradition of serving for only two terms, or eight years.

reelected in 1936, 1940, and finally, in 1944. As a reaction against Franklin Roosevelt's four-term presidency, the Twenty-second Amendment was passed in 1951. It set term limits for a president. Now a president could not be elected to more than two terms.

It is important to note that there has always been a peaceful transfer of power after each close election, regardless of who won. There were no riots and no calls for the National Guard. The same was true when George W. Bush finally took the oath of office as the forty-third president. But the 2000 presidential election was, nonetheless, like no other in American history.

3

The Road to the Supreme Court

There was no immediate winner after Election Day 2000. Al Gore had more popular votes nationwide than George W. Bush, but neither he nor Bush had enough electoral votes to become the next president. Each candidate needed to win Florida's twenty-five electoral votes. Florida, like most other states, had a winner-takes-all election policy. That meant Florida's slate of electors would vote for the candidate with the greatest number of popular votes in the state. On November 7, the original machine count of the nearly 6 million popular votes in Florida showed that Bush was ahead by 1,784 votes. But his lead, according to state law, was too small to make him the confirmed winner.

The automatic recount in Florida (required by state law) took place the next day. It showed that Bush again won the popular vote in the state—this time, by a 327-vote lead. But Gore would not admit defeat because he claimed the machine recounts were not accurate. He asked for hand recounts—but in only four Florida counties that were heavily Democratic. He also wanted the votes from these recounts added to the official state total. This was despite the fact that the state deadline to confirm all votes had passed. The battle was on.

Gore, Bush, and their supporters took to the courts to try to officially win the race in Florida. The courts had to sort out which ballots were actual legal votes in Florida's

George H. Bush, the father of George W. Bush, became president on January 20, 1989.

troublesome ballot systems. They also had to decide which of two Florida election deadlines for confirmation of all votes was legal.

Bush's father, himself a former president, downplayed the legal challenges by calling them "bumps in the road."[1] But the wins and losses of the Florida recount battle were taking a toll on the nation. With the ups and downs of court decisions, how could everyone agree that any Florida vote totals were fair and accurate? Then, too, the court battles only seemed to delay the answer to the central question: Who would be the next president? For weeks there seemed to be no end in sight to the stalemate.

Legal Battles Begin

At least forty-two lawsuits resulted from the Florida election deadlock. (The party bringing a lawsuit is the plaintiff. The party being sued is the defendant.) For the most part, the different lawsuits filed by Bush, Gore, and their supporters included these related challenges in Florida:

- To continue or halt partial hand recounts of ballots

- To extend the November 14 deadline for state confirmation of votes and to add hand recounts to the official state vote totals

- To throw out "butterfly" ballots

- To throw out questionable overseas absentee ballots

- To throw out the new November 26 deadline for state confirmation of votes; and to throw out the hand recount totals taken after the November 14 deadline

The first lawsuit was filed on November 11. The last major case was decided on December 12. So, at one time or another, Bush and Gore each had legal wins and setbacks on these issues. With each setback, their lawyers filed an appeal. (An appeal is a request by one of the parties in a lawsuit to have a higher court review a lower court's ruling on a case.) As a result, many of the lawsuits wound their way through the legal system. They went from lower courts to appeals courts. Then some cases went on to the highest court in the state—the Florida Supreme Court. Finally, two cases went on to the highest court in the nation—the United States Supreme Court.

The Florida Supreme Court made critical rulings in two key cases. One was in the *Palm Beach County Canvassing Board* v. *Harris* case on November 21. Bush appealed the rulings of that case to the United States Supreme Court. On December 4, this court issued a decision in the Bush case, called *Bush* v. *Palm Beach County Canvassing Board.* Bush also appealed the rulings that the state's highest court made on December 8 in the *Gore* v. *Harris* case. On December 9, the United States Supreme Court put the state court's rulings on hold in that second Bush case, called *Bush* v. *Gore.* It issued a historic decision in that case on December 12.

Issue of Partial Hand Recounts

Gore wanted hand recounts of punch-card ballots. He claimed the machines were faulty because they discounted punch-card ballots that had hanging chads. (These were the undervotes.) For Gore, it meant that the machines actually missed real votes. He did not need to file a lawsuit to take this action. As a presidential candidate, Gore had the legal right under Florida law (as did Bush) to ask any county for a hand recount.

Three days after the election, Gore made a critical decision in his quest to gain votes in Florida. He asked only the election supervisors in Volusia, Palm Beach, Broward, and Miami-Dade counties to do hand recounts. There were tens of thousands of votes at stake in these four heavily Democratic counties. If Gore gained enough of these votes, he could wipe out Bush's slim lead.

Bush chose not to ask for hand recounts in any Florida counties. He already led in the state's popular votes. So his strategy was to stop the hand recounts in the four Florida counties targeted by Gore. Bush filed a lawsuit in federal court the day after Gore went to the county supervisors. (See *Siegel* v. *LePore* on page 45.) His was actually the first lawsuit in the post-election legal challenges.

Bush claimed that hand recounts were unconstitutional, and should be thrown out. Why? He argued that hand recounts were not reliable. One reason was that examiners might mishandle the punch-card ballots, and possibly change the voters' selections. Another reason was that all examiners did not use the same standards for judging whether a ballot clearly showed a voter's intent. So, it meant that all the ballots (and the voters who cast the ballots) were not being treated equally. This treatment went against the Equal Protection Clause in the Constitution. (See Chapter 4 for a full argument of the Equal Protection Clause.) The rulings on the *Siegel* v. *LePore* case are as follows:

> *Siegel* v. *LePore:* On November 11, Bush and Republican supporters sued Theresa LePore (of Palm Beach) and the other county election supervisors of Volusia, Palm Beach, Broward, and Miami-Dade. On November 13, a district court judge ruled that hand recounts were not so unreliable. He refused to stop the hand recounts in these counties. Bush appealed the ruling. On December 6, an appeals court also ruled against Bush.[2]

Progress of Hand Recounts in Four Florida Counties

How did the four county election supervisors respond to Gore's request for hand recounts? These counties had a combined total of 1.8 million ballots. Obviously, it would take a great deal of time to count all these ballots by hand. So, at first, the officials agreed to conduct hand recounts in sample precincts only. If the results showed few changes, the counties would not go ahead with a full hand recount. The opposite would hold if there were many changes. Based on their samplings, two counties—Volusia and Palm Beach—voted for full hand recounts, while the two other counties—Broward and Miami-Dade—refused. Later, these two counties also decided to do full hand recounts.

In effect, Gore was asking the county supervisors to ignore the November 14 deadline. (This was the original deadline for official confirmation of vote totals in all Florida counties.) Some legal challenges at times barred the counties from continuing the recounts. Other legal challenges ordered them to continue. Only Volusia completed the hand recounts of all its ballots on time. Palm Beach also eventually completed a full hand recount. But because it missed the first and second deadlines (of November 26), only partial recount totals were added to the official totals. Broward and Miami-Dade managed to complete only partial hand recounts. These were the undervotes—the ballots in which the holes were not cleanly punched through to register a machine vote. In any event, the court delays cost the counties valuable time they needed to finish the recounts and to have the results added to the state's official total.

Hand Recounts				
	Started	Finished	Ballot Totals	Net Gains
Volusia	Nov. 12	Nov. 14	184,018 (full)	98 (Gore)
Palm Beach	Nov. 15	Nov. 26	425,000 (full)	215 (Gore)
Broward	Nov. 15	Nov. 25	6,686 (partial)	600 (Gore)
Miami-Dade	Nov. 20	Nov. 26	10,750 (partial)	168 (Gore)

Katherine Harris, the Secretary of State of Florida, refused to change the November 14 deadline.

Issue of November 14 Deadline to Confirm Votes

A Florida state law set the November 14 deadline for all sixty-seven counties to turn in their vote counts. Katherine Harris, the secretary of state of Florida, stuck to the deadline. (In each state, the secretary of state runs elections.) As the deadline grew near, the hand recounts in the four counties targeted by Gore were nowhere near completion. Yet, Harris, who had the power to change the deadline, refused

47

to do so. Her decision meant that the results of most of the hand recounts would not be included in the official state totals.

The Democrats, not surprisingly, found fault with Harris's ruling. They claimed that she was playing politics in favor of her candidate, George W. Bush. (Katherine Harris, a Republican, had worked for George W. Bush's presidential campaign.) Volusia and Palm Beach counties, joined by Gore and his supporters, challenged her decision in state court. On November 14, Judge Terry Lewis upheld Harris's deadline. At this time, Bush led by 300 popular votes. (This total reflected the automatic machine recount required by state law.)

Gore also challenged Harris's decision to refuse late totals of hand recounts. On November 17, Judge Lewis again ruled against Gore. Gore went back to court. What followed was to become one of the key appeals cases before the Florida Supreme Court that led to the historic *Bush* v. *Gore* case before the United States Supreme Court.

Florida Supreme Court Extends Original Deadline

Gore, the Florida Democratic Party, Volusia County, and Palm Beach County each appealed Judge Lewis's rulings. The appeals wound up in the Florida Supreme Court. They were combined into one case called *Palm Beach County Canvassing Board* v. *Harris*. (See page 50.)

The Florida Supreme Court wrestled with the issue of accepting vote totals from hand recounts after the November 14 deadline. The court studied two sections of a Florida election law that seemed to contradict one another on the deadline issue. (There was no separate state election law deadline for hand recount returns to be added to machine recount totals.) A 1951 section of the law said that any counties that missed the deadline "shall" be ignored. A revised 1989 chapter of the law included a section that said late returns "may" be ignored. To determine which of the

Justices of the Florida Supreme Court (from left): R. Fred Lewis, Harry Lee Anstead, Leander J. Shaw, Jr., Chief Justice Charles T. Wells, Major B. Harding, Barbara J. Pariente, and Peggy A. Quince.

two sections was binding, the court needed to decide what the Florida lawmakers had in mind. The rulings by the Florida Supreme Court on the deadline issue are as follows:

> *Palm Beach County Canvassing Board* v. *Harris:* On November 17, the Florida Supreme Court blocked Harris from confirming the November 14 vote totals. It wanted to first hear arguments from the Gore and Bush camps. Then, on November 21, the court decided that the more recent "may" section of the Florida election law better reflected the wishes of the state lawmakers. So, in a 7–0 decision, the court ruled to extend the deadline to November 26. The extra time was given so that three counties (Broward, Palm Beach, and Miami-Dade) could complete their recounts. Also, the court said that their new totals (of 1.7 million ballots) had to be included in the final state tally. Bush's lead then fell from 930 votes (which, by this time, included absentee ballots) to 537 votes. Bush appealed the ruling to the United States Supreme Court on November 22.[3]

United States Supreme Court Steps In

Bush asked the nation's highest court to overturn the Florida Supreme Court's ruling of November 21 in the *Palm Beach* v. *Harris* case. He argued that this state court violated the Constitution and federal law concerning the naming of presidential electors and the timetable for doing so. (A federal law is one that is created and passed by the United States Congress.)

This was the first time in American history that a

presidential candidate asked the high court to decide a dispute over election results. On November 24, the United States Supreme Court agreed to hear his appeal. The case before it was called *Bush* v. *Palm Beach County Canvassing Board.*[4] The Justices heard the case on December 1.

Then, on December 4, the United States Supreme Court issued a unanimous opinion in this case. It found that the reasoning for the Florida Supreme Court's ruling that allowed selective hand recounts after the original deadline was "unclear."[5] But, at this point, it did not find the ruling unlawful. The Court remanded, or sent back, the case to the state court to explain its ruling.

Why did the United States Supreme Court even bother to hear the case if it was not prepared at that time to rule on the federal issue? The federal issue was whether the state court wrongfully took over the power of state lawmakers to establish a voting system for deciding Florida's slate of electors. The nation's highest court wanted to make sure that the state court had not violated that law.

Now the question was whether the Florida Supreme Court would clearly state the reasons for its decision to the satisfaction of the United States Supreme Court. This challenge could possibly wind up either saving or rejecting the votes Gore picked up after the original deadline of November 14. But the Florida Supreme Court needed to respond before the December 12 federal deadline. Federal law, or a law passed by the U.S. Congress, requires that all

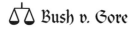

The nine justices of the Supreme Court hear cases in the Supreme Court Building on Capitol Hill.

legal problems over electoral votes be settled by this date. This law allows for a safe cushion of time between that date and December 18—the date when the official slate of electors in each state cast their votes for president and vice president. (See Chapter 4.)

Issue of Butterfly Ballots

Some Palm Beach voters sued in court to have the butterfly ballot thrown out because of its confusing design. (Of the 19,000 butterfly ballots cast, about 6,000 were contested.) They wanted a new election in the county. There were originally seven separate cases on this issue. On December 1, 2000, the Florida Supreme Court ruled that the design of the butterfly ballot was legal. The ruling was a setback for Gore.

Issue of Overseas Absentee Ballots

Voters who did not live in the Unites States at the time of the election sent in overseas absentee ballots. Florida law allowed these voters up to ten extra days after Election Day to get their ballots in. By November 18, the addition of these ballots pushed Bush's lead over Gore to 930 votes. Gore supporters sued in two Florida counties to have the overseas absentee ballots thrown out because they believed that the ballots had been tampered with. The two major cases on this issue are as follows:

Jacobs v. *Seminole County Canvassing Board:* Harry Jacobs, a lawyer and Democratic supporter, filed this lawsuit on November 27. He claimed that Republicans unlawfully added voter registration numbers to the 4,000 absentee ballot applications. These were mainly ballots from military men and women serving overseas. Some of the people were serving on ships, so they were not able to get post office marks on their envelopes. Jacobs wanted all 15,000 absentee ballots thrown out. (Bush had won the absentee ballots in this heavily Republican county. However, Gore did not actively support this lawsuit. His public position was to count every vote, not to throw out votes.) The trial began on December 6. On December 8, circuit court Judge Nikki Ann Clark ruled against Jacobs. On appeal, on December 12, the Florida Supreme Court upheld Judge Clark's decision.[6]

Taylor v. *Martin County Canvassing Board:* Ronald Taylor filed this lawsuit on December 3. As in the Seminole County case, he and other Democrats wanted the court to reject Martin County's 9,773 absentee ballots for the same reason. (Bush had won more than 6,000 absentee votes in this county.) On December 8, Judge Terry P. Lewis ruled in favor of the Bush defendants. On appeal, on December 12, the Florida Supreme Court upheld Judge Lewis's decision.[7]

Florida Secretary of State Harris Under Attack Again

On November 26, Florida Secretary of State Harris once again (by order of the Florida Supreme Court) confirmed the state's vote totals. This time, however, Bush beat Gore in the popular vote in Florida by 537 votes. More importantly, it meant that Bush *officially won* Florida's twenty-five electoral votes.

Yet the battle was not over. Gore (as allowed by Florida law) contested Harris's confirmation of vote totals. That meant Gore was also contesting her confirmation of Bush as the winner in Florida. His major case on this issue, as described below, was *Gore v. Harris*.

> *Gore v. Harris* (circuit court contest): Gore sued in state court on November 27, 2000. He contested the November 14 official vote results in Palm Beach and Miami-Dade counties (as well as Nassau County). Officials in Miami-Dade County had stopped the hand recounts on November 22. They had realized they could not meet the new November 26 deadline.

THE UPS AND DOWNS OF BUSH'S LEAD IN FLORIDA[8]		
	Date	Total
Election Day	Nov. 7	1,784
Unofficial recount	Nov. 9	327
Reported to Harris	Nov. 14	300
With overseas ballots	Nov. 18	930
Confirmed by Harris	Nov. 26	537
With partial recounts added	Dec. 8	193
Unofficial renewed recount	Dec. 9	177
U.S. Supreme Court ruling	Dec. 13	537

Also, Palm Beach County had missed the new November 26 deadline by two hours. Harris rejected the results of the county's hand recount of about 19,000 butterfly ballots. Instead, on November 26, she confirmed the November 14 totals for both Palm Beach and Miami-Dade. Gore wanted Judge N. Sanders Sauls to order that the hand recounts of the undervotes in Miami-Dade and Palm Beach counties should continue. But, on December 4, Judge Sauls ruled against him.[9]

Gore v. *Harris* (Florida Supreme Court contest): Gore appealed Judge Sauls's ruling to the Florida Supreme Court on December 6. On December 8, the state's highest court decided in favor of Gore. It ordered a hand recount of 9,000 "undervote" ballots in Miami-Dade County. It also ruled that Gore gained 383 popular votes from Miami-Dade and Palm Beach from earlier partial hand recounts. Now Bush led by only 193 votes in the state. This was a major victory for Gore. The ruling challenged Bush's newly confirmed lead of 537 votes.[10]

Also, the Florida Supreme Court went a step further than even Gore would have hoped for. It strongly urged Judge Sauls to order a hand recount of all 45,000 undervotes (that were not counted by hand earlier) throughout the state. Bush filed an emergency application to the United States Supreme Court to stop these recounts. This action set into motion a series of events that would, at last, decide the election. (See the last section in this chapter.)

Republican Backup Plan

Meanwhile, Florida Republicans lawmakers had a backup plan if the courts failed to secure Bush's victory. (They controlled the state's House and Senate.) On December 3, these lawmakers threatened to name their own set of presidential electors for Bush. (Remember, state lawmakers have the power, under the Constitution, to determine the method of appointing their electors.) They would go by the originally confirmed election results, in which Bush led Gore by 537 popular votes.

The lawmakers would do so, they said, if Gore's legal challenges to the original set of electors for Bush were not resolved by December 12. By federal law, that was the deadline for final confirmation of votes in all the states. Also, by that date, there should be no remaining problems about the identity of a state's slate of presidential electors. (These conditions needed to be met in order to pave the way for state electors to actually cast their votes on December 18.) What if Florida failed to solve its electoral problems in time? Then its original slate of twenty-five electors for Bush would not be recognized on January 6. That was when the United States Congress was to meet to officially tally the electoral votes of the Electoral College nationwide.

What if Gore won the court battles on the hand recount issues in Florida? Then there would be two opposing slates of electors for Florida—one Republican slate for Bush and one Democratic slate for Gore. If that happened, it would be up to the United States Congress to choose between the double set of Florida electors. (Remember, in the election of 1876, four states sent double sets of electoral votes to Congress. A special panel was set up to select one of the candidates to be the new president.) Now it would take a simple majority of both houses of Congress, where the odds were in Bush's favor.[11]

Public Reactions to Florida Election Battles

Because of the importance of the office of president, a presidential race is usually followed with great interest at home and around the world. During the 2000 election battles in Florida, some nations around the world watched with some degree of worry. After all, the United States served as a democratic model of fair and open elections and peaceful transition of government. Did Americans worry, too, about the court actions? The following surveys show that they grew less patient as time went by.

- November 12: Neither candidate should challenge the first recount of Florida votes in the courts.[12]

- November 30: 62 percent wanted the United States Supreme Court to settle the Florida deadlock.[13]

- December 3: Public opinion on Bush's behavior was split. However, 65 percent of Americans did not approve of Gore's court challenges to gain the presidency.[14]

- December 6: Six out of ten Americans felt Gore should give up.[15]

Acting Presidential

What were Gore and Bush doing while the legal challenges were playing out in the courts? It was important for each of them to "look" presidential because the eyes of the world were sizing them up. They had to show leadership abilities, decision-making abilities, and the ability to withstand pressure. So, the two candidates took part in various kinds of role-playing.

Gore and Bush held strategy meetings with their aides. They held press conferences to appeal their positions directly to the people. But each candidate also made sure he was photographed in relaxed surroundings. It was also important for each of them to not appear desperate to win.

By November 27, Al Gore greatly needed to gain public support for his continued battle for the presidency. Gore said in a televised speech that his fight for votes was necessary to defend democracy. "This is America," he said. "When votes are cast, we count them."[16] He was referring to his push to count by hand the thousands of Florida ballots that the machines rejected.

George W. Bush, however, did not appear to be worried. What did he do in the days leading to the historic decision by the United States Supreme Court on December 12? Bush took a bold, confident step. He was seen hard at work

While waiting for the Supreme Court decision, Bush continued getting ready for his presidency.

picking his White House staff. Gore, meanwhile, kept a low profile.

The Clock Stopped Temporarily

On December 9, the United States Supreme Court stepped into the Florida vote challenges a second time. This time, it granted Bush's request to stop the hand recounts of the more than 45,000 "undervote" ballots in the entire state until it would hear his appeal. (The Florida Supreme Court had given that recount order in the *Gore* v. *Harris* case on

December 8.) The nation's highest court then scheduled to hear oral arguments in this *Bush* v. *Gore* case in two days. That meant lawyers for Bush and Gore would argue the issues of the case before the nine Justices of the Court.

Ordering a halt to the recount meant that the court issued a stay order. A stay order has two main requirements. It requires the votes of at least five of the nine justices on the court. (The Court's decision to stop the Florida recounts was 5 to 4.) It also requires an emergency situation that threatens permanent harm to the petitioner. Bush, the petitioner in this case, made a successful argument on that issue. He argued that the results of hand recounts were not legal. Also, he argued that the added votes from these recounts changed the legal outcome of the November 7 election in Florida. This development, Bush claimed, harmed his rightful chances of winning the national election.

Some legal experts said there was another reason for the Court's decision to grant Bush's appeal. They suggested that another matter might have upset the high court. It was the fact that the Florida Supreme Court had not as yet responded to its December 4 order in the *Bush* v. *Palm Beach County Canvassing Board* case.[17] In that ruling, the United States Supreme Court had asked the state court to explain why it changed the election deadline to allow new recounts.

The stay order by the United States Supreme Court came one day after the statewide hand recounts began. It brought election workers to an immediate halt. A supervisor

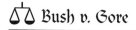

Supreme Court Justice Antonin Scalia wrote the concurring opinion of the Court, stating that George W. Bush had the greater chance of winning the *Bush* v. *Gore* case.

of elections rushed into the Leon County courthouse. He told a clerk to pack up the ballots. Similar scenes took place in county after county in Florida.[18] The seesaw effect of the dueling supreme courts made for dizzying emotions. One day Gore had reason to hope; the next day Bush was joyous.

Justice Scalia wrote a concurring opinion to the Court's Order. In it, he boldly stated that Bush had a great chance of winning the *Bush* v. *Gore* case.[19] So, clearly, Gore would face an uphill battle before the Court. Did Justice Scalia also forecast the Court's final decision in this case? The answer would be made public in three days. What the Court's ruling did make immediately clear was that it would decide who won the presidential election. Now there was no other legal action in sight to begin the recount again. The order by the United States Supreme Court could not be appealed.

It was now thirty-three days after the November election—and counting. As the December 12 deadline to name Florida's electors drew nearer, the clock began to tick louder than ever.

4

The Case for George W. Bush

George W. Bush asked the United States Supreme Court to step in and stop the hand recounts. He claimed the Florida Supreme Court's rulings in the *Gore* v. *Harris* case on December 8, 2000, raised federal issues. The United States Supreme Court granted Bush a stay order a day later (on a Saturday). In addition to stopping the hand recounts, the Court went one better. It also treated the stay order as a petition for a *writ of certiorari.* (This is an order from the Court to hear the arguments of a case.) Then, the Court immediately granted that petition.

For a speedy process, the Court asked the lawyers for Bush and Gore to provide legal briefs and responses to those briefs within a couple of days. (A brief is a written argument in a legal case.) It asked lawyers for both sides to focus on issues involving violations of the Constitution. Both sides filed briefs as quickly as Sunday, December 10. (Justice Thomas would later comment that "computers change everything. No way could we have done the case over the weekend" without receiving or reading briefs online.)[1]

The case of *Bush* v. *Gore* was underway. This would be the third and last time the United States Supreme Court ruled on issues stemming from the 2000 presidential election. The Court had never before taken a case involving a presidential election in its entire 210-year history.

The Courthouse Drama

The United States Supreme Court heard oral arguments in the *Bush* v. *Gore* case on December 11. On the Republican side, Theodore Olson argued for Bush. (Florida Secretary of State Harris was also a party to the proceedings. That was because this case stemmed from the *Gore* v. *Harris* case. Joseph Klock argued for Harris.)

About a thousand protestors gathered outside the Supreme Court building on December 11. Chiseled on the white marble building are the words: "Equal Justice Under the Law." Many protestors gathered nearby and waved their own printed signs. Hundreds of union members in support of Gore held signs that read: "This is America. Count every vote."[2] Bush supporters competed with their own signs, which said such things as, "Five to four, no more Gore."[3]

Tensions ran high inside the courthouse, too. But the

mood was quiet. There were only fifty seats set aside for the general public. The remaining seats were reserved for members of Congress, reporters, selected lawyers, and court workers. Neither Bush nor Gore attended the oral arguments, but three of Gore's four children did. (Bush stayed at the governor's mansion in Austin, Texas. Gore stayed at the vice president's official home in Washington, D.C.)

At about 11 A.M., the gavel struck, signalling the entrance of the nine Justices. The Justices wore black robes and sat down in high-backed leather chairs. Questions by the Justices showed their concerns. (They asked a total of

While *Bush* v. *Gore* was being heard in the Supreme Court building, protestors gathered outside to make their opinions known.

194 questions during the entire hearing, which lasted ninety-seven minutes.) They asked each lawyer, in turn, to explain the federal issues of the case. (Keep in mind that without the existence of federal issues, the Florida election battles would be outside of the Court's reach. Instead, they could be settled in either of two ways: The ballot recounts would be completed as ordered by the state supreme court; or the state lawmakers could vote in their slate of electors—which they were already poised to do.)

Some of the Justices were concerned about the different standards for counting ballots in Florida counties. Others wondered if there was enough time to hand count the remaining undervotes. At times during the oral arguments, the rulings by the Florida Supreme Court in both key cases—*Palm Beach County Canvassing Board* v. *Harris* and *Gore* v. *Harris*—were at issue.

Florida Supreme Court's Late Reply

Sure enough, the issue of the Florida Supreme Court's lack of a response came up during oral arguments. (Remember, on December 4, the United States Supreme Court ordered this state court to explain its ruling of November 21 in the *Palm Beach County Canvassing Board* v. *Harris* case. In that case, the state court allowed the hand recounts to continue.) Justice Sandra Day O'Connor remarked that this state court "seemed to kind of bypass" the order, and that was "troublesome" to her.[4]

In fact, the Florida Supreme Court did respond to the order. But it was hours later on that same day of the oral arguments in the *Bush* v. *Gore* case. Why did Florida's highest court take a week to reply? It explained that it had waited for follow-up briefs from the lawyers in order to proceed in the *Gore* v. *Harris* case.

Regardless, the Florida Supreme Court defended its ruling. It insisted it had not made new law. Rather, it had interpreted Florida's election law. What was the conclusion? This court refused to make any further rulings. It left it up to the state lawmakers to deal with the problems arising from their election law. It also restored the November 26 deadline. That meant this state court would allow the addition of late recount totals to the state tally.

Justices' Public Face

During oral arguments in a case, the Justices put on a public face to only a select few. They never allow television or still cameras to record the hearings. Why? Justice Kennedy said it teaches the lesson that the Court is "different from the other branches of government."[5]

The Justices, however, usually release audiotapes of the oral arguments months later. But this time they did allow the immediate release of these tapes to the public. That was because the *Bush* v. *Gore* tapes were of great interest to many people. How did the public react to the hearings? Some people who heard the Justices for the very first time felt that the

Court's longstanding air of mystery was unveiled. Why? They got to hear the Justices fire off serious questions in rapid order. They also got to hear them crack jokes and laugh. In short, the public came to know them in a somewhat personal way. Now they viewed the Justices not only as wise and powerful but also as ordinary people much like themselves.

Bush's Constitutional Arguments

Now it was time for George W. Bush to make his case. Bush's main arguments represent those raised in oral arguments and in the petitioner's brief. They are also represented in the Court's written decision in this case. In Bush's brief, his lawyers described the general thrust of the Florida Supreme Court's decision as "a recipe for electoral chaos."[6] In general, Bush argued that the Florida hand recounts should stop because they were in violation

Supreme Court Justice Sandra Day O'Connor had issues with the state court's procedures regarding the *Palm Beach County Canvassing Board* v. *Harris* case.

of the Constitution and federal laws. He presented two main issues:

1. *Did the Florida Supreme Court create new standards to resolve the outcome of a presidential election?*[7]

Bush argued that the state court did create new standards when it changed deadlines and rules after the election took place. (On November 21, 2000, in the Palm Beach case, the Florida Supreme Court pushed back the state deadline for confirmation of votes from November 14 to November 26 to allow hand recounts.) As such, Bush argued, the state court violated Article II of the Constitution.

> **Article II (Section 1, Clause 2) of the Constitution** says that the states shall name the electors at the direction of their lawmakers. That means the states (and the state lawmakers), are responsible for choosing electors. How so? The state lawmakers craft the process of selecting electors and make it into law. It also means that the state courts are not involved in the selection of electors.

Bush claimed that the Florida Supreme Court ignored a state election law that set November 14 as the deadline. He argued that Article II prevented this state court from making a ruling on the deadline issue. This law, Bush argued, did not allow for late vote counts. Therefore, he claimed that the state court violated Article II when it "substituted its judgment for that of the [state lawmakers]."[8]

Bush also brought up an argument that was designed to irritate the Justices. It was about the state court's ruling of December 8 in the *Gore* v. *Harris* case. (In that ruling, the Florida Supreme Court ordered that Gore votes gained from earlier partial hand recounts in Miami-Dade and Palm Beach had to be added to Gore's total.) Bush argued that the ruling was based on the court's ruling of November 21. But the United States Supreme Court, Bush pointed out, had already thrown out that earlier ruling. Therefore, the state court, he charged, deliberately disobeyed the highest court in the nation.

> 2. *Did the use of hand recounts that lacked standards violate the Due Process and Equal Protection Clauses in the Fourteenth Amendment to the Constitution?*[9]

This second issue dealt with the Florida Supreme Court's ruling to conduct hand recounts without the use of specific standards. That is, standards to decide whether the punch-card ballots with indentations or with hanging chads were legal votes. In Florida, different counties had different standards for recounting ballots. Even different recount teams within a county used different standards.

> **Fourteenth Amendment:** Section 1 guarantees the rights to "due process" and "equal protection." It is "an important way through which the federal government enforces the values of basic human rights and equal protection on state governments."[10]

The Due Process Clause: It is the right to have laws applied fairly to all persons. It applies to state government and state courts.

The Equal Protection Clause: It is the right to equal protection of laws. (It was originally passed to guarantee equal protection to freed black slaves.) That means the states must apply laws equally and fairly to all people.

On the issue of the Due Process Clause, Bush claimed that the Florida Supreme Court violated it in several key ways. One way, he said, was that the state court did not honor the Florida election law that already existed. Bush argued that, as a result, the election outcome would be based on "'rules' [made by the state court, and not the state lawmakers] that were not in place when the votes were cast."[11] This state court, Bush argued, also failed "to provide and apply clear and consistent guidelines" to oversee the hand recounts.[12] Finally, Bush said the state court failed to allow him and others to contest ballot outcomes. These actions, therefore, were in violation of the Due Process Clause.

Bush claimed that the Florida Supreme Court also violated the Equal Protection Clause when it ordered hand recounts without the benefit of standards. He said that meant that the same types of ballots in different counties would be counted differently. In effect, Bush argued, Florida voters would be treated differently in various counties; such unequal treatment violated the voters' constitutional right to equal protection of the Florida election law.

Bush's Federal Arguments

What federal law did Bush claim that the Florida Supreme Court violated? Basically, Bush applied the first issue (see above) to a violation of the federal election law as well. The question presented was as follows:

> *Did the Florida Supreme Court create new standards to resolve the outcome of a presidential election, thereby violating Title III, Section 5 of the United States Code?*[13]

Title III, Section 5 of the Unites States Code: This is a section of a federal law that deals with the selection of presidential electors. It says that the process for selecting electors must be spelled out in laws passed *before* Election Day. It also requires that any problems dealing with a state's slate of presidential electors must be resolved by December 12.

Bush explained that Congress voted in Section 5 of the federal election law to avoid a repeat of the problems of the presidential election of 1876. (See Chapter 2.) Section 5, he explained, provides a "safe harbor" for Congress to accept a state's electoral votes. Bush said it provides "certainty and finality" to presidential elections.[14] He claimed it also represents Congress's will that rules for resolving election challenges "cannot be changed once the voters have gone to the polls."[15]

On December 8 (in the *Gore* v. *Harris* case), the Florida Supreme Court ordered a hand recount of undervotes in Miami-Dade County. It also strongly urged the same action for all the counties in the state. That was only four days before the federal deadline of December 12. Bush claimed that this ruling created new standards that threatened to overturn already confirmed election results. Therefore, he argued, the state court's ruling also violated this federal election law.

In closing, Bush asked the United States Supreme Court to reverse the judgment of the state court's ruling in the *Gore* v. *Harris* case. Next, it was Al Gore's turn to argue his case.

5

The Case for Al Gore

Remember that George W. Bush, not Al Gore, had brought the complaint about the Florida hand recounts to the United States Supreme Court. That meant Gore was the respondent, or defendant, in the *Bush* v. *Gore* case. On December 11, 2000, Gore's lawyer (as well as lawyers for Bush and Harris) had a chance to argue his case before the Justices. This time, David Boies argued for Gore. (Lawrence Tribe had represented Gore before the United States Supreme Court in the *Bush* v. *Palm Beach County Canvassing Board* case on December 1.)

Boies was also Gore's trial lawyer in the Florida lower court cases. The focus of the arguments in the *Bush* v. *Gore* case would be mainly on Florida election law. So Boies, who was more experienced than Tribe in this area, took on the task. It was only his second time before the Court.

Gore's Constitutional Arguments

Now it was time for Al Gore to make his case. He responded to the questions posed by George W. Bush. Gore's main arguments, as follows, represent those raised in oral arguments and in the respondent's brief. They are also represented in the Court's written decision in this case. In general, Gore argued that no constitutional issues were involved in this case. Therefore, he said, the rulings made by Florida Supreme Court should stand.

1. *Did the Florida Supreme Court create new standards to resolve the outcome of a presidential election?*[1]

Gore claimed, "Article II provides no basis to override the Florida Supreme Court."[2] Therefore, he argued, this state court did not take power away from the state lawmakers. He also argued that the Florida Supreme Court did not create new standards when it changed deadlines and rules after the election took place.

David Boies acted as Gore's attorney in the *Bush* v. *Gore* case.

76

Rather, it interpreted the Florida election law, as was its right. Gore also explained that Florida did not have a separate election law that contained all the requirements for the selection of presidential electors. But, he argued, Article II does not require it. For these reasons, Gore said, the Florida Supreme Court did not violate Article II of the Constitution.

2. *Did the use of hand recounts that lacked standards violate the Due Process and Equal Protection Clauses in the Fourteenth Amendment of the Constitution?*[3]

On the issue of the Due Process Clause, Gore claimed that the Florida Supreme Court did go by the Florida election law. He argued that Florida lawmakers did not bar this state court's function to interpret and apply it. He noted that they gave the Florida Supreme Court the power to do so under the state's constitution. Therefore, Gore argued, the state court did not make new standards. In addition, Gore said that the recount procedures provided a way of defending a person's right to vote.[4]

On the issue of the Equal Protection Clause, Gore argued that the Florida Supreme Court should not be faulted for not providing more specific standards for inspectors who recounted ballots by hand, other than what the state law said. The only requirement set by the state's lawmakers was a rather general one. It said that ballot inspectors needed to find "a clear indication of the intent of the voter."[5] (This requirement was not limited to the state of Florida. In fact, a total of thirty-three states used this standard.)[6] If the state court had gone further, Gore argued, then Bush would also have faulted it for providing "new" standards, which is unconstitutional.

Gore's Federal Arguments

Gore raised the issue of federalism in general. He argued that *state* law regulates elections and the selection of electors. So the *federal* system, including the United States Supreme Court, should not be involved in the Florida election. The specific federal issue before the Court, and Gore's arguments about it are as follows:

> *Did the Florida Supreme Court create new standards to resolve the outcome of a presidential election, thereby violating Title III, Section 5 of the United States Code?*[7]

Gore claimed that the Florida Supreme Court's decision of December 8 was in agreement with this section of the federal election law. (Remember, Section 5 says that the process for selecting electors must be spelled out in laws passed *before* Election Day. It also requires that any problems dealing with a state's slate of presidential electors must be resolved by December 12.)

Gore argued that Section 5 has a "narrow purpose." That purpose is to set up "only a safe harbor from a challenge in Congress [on December 18] to a state's slate of electors."[8] He also argued that the state court's decision did not change Florida law. Therefore, he said, the decision did not affect Florida's right to the safe harbor of the federal election law. For these reasons, Gore said, Bush's argument on this question "fails."

In closing, Gore asked the United States Supreme Court to uphold the judgment of the state court's ruling in the *Gore* v. *Harris* case. In addition, he asked the Court to lift the stay order that stopped the hand recounts.

Both George W. Bush and Al Gore had spoken. Now it was up to the United States Supreme Court to decide the case. How would it rule? Whose arguments—Bush's or Gore's—would convince the Court?

6

The Decision

The United States Supreme Court had heard oral arguments by the lawyers in the *Bush* v. *Gore* case on December 11, 2000. Afterward, the Justices discussed the issues of the case alone in a conference room. Then they returned to their individual offices to research and write. Typically, the Justices may meet again informally in pairs or in small groups to talk over the issues even further. Final touches are then added to the majority opinion. Then concurring (in agreement) and dissenting (in disagreement) opinions are added to it. All this work takes time. But this case required a speedy outcome, and the Justices did not delay.

The Court issued a decision in the *Bush* v. *Gore* case at about ten o'clock on the very next night, December 12. It was, in effect, a two-part decision. The first part—on whether the Court found fault with one or more of the

After hearing the oral arguments, the Justices discussed the issue in their conference room.

issues—represented a 7 to 2 majority. The second part—on how to resolve the problem of what the Court found to be at fault—represented a narrow 5 to 4 majority.

Five separate written opinions were added to the Court's decision. One was by several Justices who agreed with the 7 to 2 majority decision but included additional reasons. But the four other opinions revealed the 5 to 4 split on the separate issue of how to resolve the problem. The Justices who wrote and signed these separate opinions disagreed with all or parts of the Court's decision.

81

The 7 to 2 Majority Decision

The Court's ruling was labeled *per curiam* ("by the court"). That meant the Court spoke with one voice rather than by a single justice. Therefore, the thirteen-page ruling was not signed.

In the 7 to 2 majority opinion, the Justices were careful to point out they did not seek out the task of hearing this case. They noted their respect for the "Constitution's design to leave the selection of the President to the people, through their [lawmakers], and to the political [parties]."[1]

Nevertheless, the Justices said they had to step in. They explained that Bush and Gore took their election disputes to the courts. Therefore, it was the Court's "unsought" duty "to resolve the federal and constitutional issues the judicial system has been forced to confront."[2]

The stakes were very high in the *Bush* v. *Gore* case. The winner would most likely be the next president of the United States. At issue in this case was whether the Florida Supreme Court's ruling on December 8, 2000, was faulty. This state court had ordered hand recounts of all "undervote" ballots in Florida. Three important questions hung in the balance.[3] (The same questions discussed in briefs and in oral arguments.)

1. *Did the Florida Supreme Court create new standards to resolve the outcome of a presidential election?* If so, it violated Article II of the Constitution.

2. Did the use of hand recounts that lacked standards violate the Equal Protection and Due Process Clauses in the Fourteenth Amendment of the Constitution?

3. Did the Florida Supreme Court create new standards to resolve the outcome of a presidential election, thereby violating Title III of the United States Code, Section 5?

Of the three questions before the Court, seven of the nine Justices agreed that the unequal treatment of the ballot recount process in Florida *did* violate the Fourteenth

From left to right, the Supreme Court Justices who presided over the *Bush v. Gore* case are: (seated) Antonin Scalia, John Paul Stevens, Chief Justice William Rehnquist, Sandra Day O'Connor, and Anthony M. Kennedy; (standing) Ruth Bader Ginsburg, David H. Souter, Clarence Thomas, and Stephen G. Breyer.

Amendment's Equal Protection Clause. The seven Justices included Chief Justice Rehnquist and Justices O'Connor, Scalia, Kennedy, Souter, Thomas, and Breyer. (The majority decision was unsigned. But the names of the seven Justices could be identified through clues in the concurring and dissenting opinions.) These Justices pointed out three Equal Protection problems:

- The Florida Supreme Court failed to include the overvotes in the hand recounts.

- All the ballots were recounted in only some counties.

- There were no specific standards to recount the ballots by hand.

The Justices applied the third problem to fair voting procedures. They reasoned that the lack of specific standards caused unequal checking of the undervote ballots. Basic to the right to vote, they said, is the "equal weight [given] to each vote and the equal [respect] owed to each voter." Therefore, the state may not "value one person's vote over that of another by the later use of this unequal treatment."[4]

For these reasons, the Court reversed the judgment of the Florida Supreme Court. That meant the hand recount of undervotes could not continue. As part of the judgment, the Court then sent the case back to the state court for further proceedings.

Additional Opinion of Chief Justice Rehnquist:
Chief Justice Rehnquist issued the only opinion concurring with the majority. He wrote that there were more reasons to reverse the Florida Supreme Court's ruling. He believed the Florida Supreme Court also violated Article II of the Constitution and Section 5 of the federal election law. Justices Scalia and Thomas joined him in this opinion.

The Dissent of the 7 to 2 Majority Opinion: The two Justices who totally disagreed with the majority opinion were Justices Ginsburg and Stevens. They did not believe the Florida Supreme Court violated any constitutional or federal laws. Justice Stevens was particularly worried about how the people would view the Court after this decision. He felt they would think the Court's decision was based on politics and not on an evenhanded reading of the law. Justice Ginsburg believed the Court should have upheld the ruling of the Florida Supreme Court out of customary respect to the state court's authority. "Federal courts defer to state high court's interpretations of their state's own laws," she said.[5]

5 to 4 Decision Not to Order a New Recount System

The Justices were divided on whether to order a new recount system in Florida. The split was 5 to 4. They disagreed on how to fix the constitutional problem of equal treatment of votes.

Five of the Justices ruled that no recounts should continue. They said that to allow hand recounts without specific standards was not an "appropriate" solution.[6] These five were Chief Justice Rehnquist and Justices O'Connor, Scalia, Kennedy, and Thomas. They also agreed that there was no time left to set new statewide standards as well as to recount the ballots before midnight on December 12. The Justices insisted that was the deadline that must be met. They explained that a federal law required the Florida lawmakers to choose the state's electors by that date. That deadline, however, was only two hours away. *So, time had simply run out.* The Court, therefore, not only reversed the state court but, in effect, stopped the hand recounts altogether.

Four other Justices, however, disagreed with the Court's solution of stopping the recounts outright. They were Justices Stevens, Souter, Ginsburg, and Breyer. They each issued separate dissenting opinions. These were attached to the Court's majority opinion. These same Justices all believed that December 18, not December 12, was the final deadline.

"The Court's concern about the December 12 deadline is misplaced," Justice Ginsburg said. "Were that date to pass, Florida would still be entitled to deliver electoral votes."[7] (In fact, Florida was not the only tardy state in the election of 2000. Only twenty-nine states met the December 12 federal deadline.)[8]

That meant the four Justices agreed with Gore that December 12 was only a "safe harbor" date for states to confirm their own electors. The purpose of meeting this

A Look Back in History

During the 1960 election, Hawaii had already officially confirmed Richard Nixon's three electors. But John Kennedy demanded a recount. A court battle followed. While a full recount was still going on, the state cast two competing sets of electoral votes—one set for Nixon and another for Kennedy. After the recount, a judge ruled that Kennedy had won by a narrow margin. When the electoral votes of all the states were counted in Congress in January, Kennedy's electoral votes from Hawaii were accepted.[9] (Kennedy won the presidential election.)

deadline was to avoid a challenge later to a state's slate of electors. December 18 was the date when the Electoral College was scheduled to cast their votes for president and vice-president. (Congress would meet on January 6 to formally count the electoral votes state by state.)

In defense of his dissenting opinion, Justice Stevens gave an example where a state (Hawaii) missed the federal deadline. That state's electoral votes were, nevertheless, counted later in Congress. It happened during the presidential election of 1960.

In their dissenting opinions, Justices Breyer and Souter offered a different solution to that of the Court's. They would send the case back to the Florida Supreme Court. They wanted the state court to order a proper recount of the votes until December 18. They believed the recounts could be completed by that date. But their opinions were part of the minority. And so their solution did not pass.

Time's Up!

The Court's decision meant that, without further recounts in Florida, the previous totals were in effect. Bush, who led in the popular votes in Florida by 537 votes, was declared the winner in that state. He was awarded the state's twenty-five electoral votes. That put him over the top. Bush now had 271 electoral votes nationwide. (That was one more than the required 270 votes.) That meant he won the presidential election. Gore, who remained with a total of 266 electoral votes, was the official loser.

For Al Gore, time was the "worst enemy."[10] He had finally run out of legal options to contest the vote totals. The United States Supreme Court, the highest court in the nation, had the final word. "It's time for me to go," Gore said.[11]

Gore Finally Admits Defeat

On December 13, Al Gore made a televised speech in which he finally admitted defeat. (More than 65 million viewers tuned in to see it). It was the day after the United States

THE CHRISTIAN SCIENCE MONITOR Bennett

Al Gore said that time was the "worst enemy" in the decision over the outcome of the presidential election of 2000.

Supreme Court handed down its decision on the *Bush* v. *Gore* case.

Gore said he had just phoned Bush to congratulate him. "I promised him that I wouldn't call him back this time," Gore added jokingly, referring to the fact that he had called Bush twice on Election Night—once to admit defeat, then again to take it back.[12]

Gore also commented on the Court's decision. "Now the U.S. Supreme Court has spoken. Let there be no doubt, while I strongly disagree with the court's decision, I accept it."[13] Gore then gave up his bid for the presidency "for the sake of our unity of the people and the strength of our democracy."[14]

Bush Finally Claims Victory

President-elect Bush had waited in Austin, Texas, for Gore to concede before addressing the nation himself. Now it was finally his time to claim victory. In an effort to unite the nation, Bush reached out to everyone in his televised speech. "I was not elected to serve one party, but to serve one nation," he said. "Whether you voted for me or not," Bush added, "I will do my best to serve your interests, and I will work to earn your respect."[15]

Congress confirmed Bush's electoral victory (of 271 electoral votes) on January 6, 2001. That meant George W. Bush was now the president-elect. (Remember, a president-elect is someone who has been elected but has not yet been

President George W. Bush was sworn in on January 20, 2001.

sworn into office.) Oddly enough, it was Vice President Gore who read the electoral vote count at a joint session of Congress. It was one of his last formal duties as president of the Senate.

Then on January 20, 2001, George W. Bush was sworn in as the forty-third president of the United States. It was an amazing feat for someone whose father had left the White House just eight years earlier. As a new president, Bush enjoyed a typical period of cooperation from the public, Congress, and the press.

Reactions to the Supreme Court Decision

Reaction to the Court's decision came swiftly. It came from voters, politicians, and the legal community. It was emotional and deeply personal. No two people expressed their opinions in quite the same way. And the points of view ranged from A to Z. In general, Bush supporters viewed the Bush victory as a sign that the legal system worked. Gore supporters viewed the Gore loss as a sign that the legal system failed.

Remember the news poll taken on November 30, 2000? (See Chapter 3.) At that time, 62 percent of those surveyed said they wanted the United States Supreme Court to settle the Florida deadlock.[16] But a news poll taken immediately after the Court's decision showed otherwise. In this later survey, 63 percent said they had less trust in the legal system than before the 2000 election. Only 20 percent said they had more trust in it.[17] That survey revealed the public's change of faith in the court system to deal with political issues.

The opinions expressed in some other interviews seemed to bear out Justice Stevens's worst fear about the Court's decision. These people did attack the image of the United States Supreme Court. They believed that the status of the Court as a highly trusted institution had been tarnished. They felt the Court's decision appeared to be politically motivated. Other people questioned whether their votes really counted after all, since the Court is not directly answerable to the people. One man expressed the idea this way: "[Gore] won the popular vote. So the people did speak, but they weren't exactly heard."[18]

Finally, two individuals expressed unique opinions that bear mention. One teacher blamed everyone involved—the candidates, the lawyers, and the courts—for just wanting to win. He wondered how they would have acted if Bush rather than Gore had been behind in the Florida vote counts. Would they have taken the "opposite view"?[19] But, perhaps, one private citizen said it best about what he thought of the long, hard-fought ordeal that put the election outcome and the nation on hold. "Let's get on to having a new president," he said.[20]

7

Where Do We Stand Today?

The decision in the *Bush* v. *Gore* case sent broad signals to the courts, lawmakers, election officials, and voters. It paved the way for voters to sue state elections officials on the grounds of the Equal Protection Clause in the Fourteenth Amendment. It exposed the weaknesses in the Florida elections laws and ballot systems.

But the broader issue was the need for voting reforms nationwide. Specific steps were necessary to achieve the goals. Would outdated voting machines and ballot systems be replaced? Could minority voters expect fair and equal treatment at the polls in future elections? Would television networks improve the way they gathered election results?

Then, too, there remained the lingering doubt, for some people, about the final vote count in Florida. Would voters and lawmakers have full confidence in President George W. Bush? How would unforeseen events harm the country but strengthen President Bush?

All States on Notice

Did the United States Supreme Court's decision in *Bush* v. *Gore*, in effect, put all the states on notice? The Court said standard rules to determine a voter's intent are both practical and "necessary."[1] But the Court said the majority decision to apply the Fourteenth Amendment's Equal Protection Clause was "limited to the present circumstances" in that case.[2]

However, many lawyers believed that the Court's narrow ruling would not stop people in other states from suing on the same grounds of equal protection. Some voters and civil rights groups, in fact, did test the Court's ruling. They believed the requirement of fair and equal voting methods and counting standards applied to all the states, not just Florida. The first such lawsuit was filed less than a month after the landmark case. To date, the Court's equal protection standard was put to the test in over a dozen lawsuits.

Election Reforms

Has the voting system improved since the 2000 election? Yes, some important steps were taken to rethink and improve voting procedures in Florida as well as nationwide. However, there never was—and still is not—a national voting system. (Two universities announced on December 14, 2000, that they would work together to develop a plan for a national voting system. They were the California and Massachusetts Institutes of Technology.)

Almost six months after the 2000 election, Florida lawmakers voted in sweeping election reforms. They spelled out standard methods for recounting votes in close elections. They did away with punch-card ballots. For future elections, Florida counties were in favor of using touch-

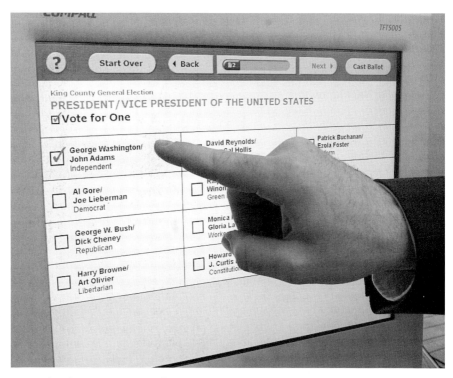

Florida counties are in favor of using touch-screen voting machines, like the one shown here, in future elections.

screen voting machines. The touch-screen system does not use paper ballots. There is no problem of overvotes with this machine because it does not accept two votes for different candidates running for the same office. These new machines cost the state a princely sum of about $32 million. To help pay for the new machines, Palm Beach County officials began selling off the old voting machines on the Internet. They also sent one of these machines for display at the Smithsonian Institution in Washington, D.C.

In June 2001, a major computer maker and an election services company teamed up to "modernize the way America votes."[3] They believe the new machines will help make voting easier. They will add up the votes faster and more reliably.

One problem, however, remains: Who can afford the new machines? For example, the cost of new voting machines in Los Angeles County was estimated at $100 million.[4] The burden is up to each state and, in turn, each county. Poorer counties with old equipment have generally had the most serious problems of voting. (Remember the problems caused by the old punch-card system in some Florida counties during the 2000 election?)

What has the national government done about election reform? Two years after the landmark decision in *Bush* v. *Gore*, Congress passed a bill to reform the election system. It is called the Help America Vote Act of 2002. It grants almost $4 billion to the states to help them replace old types of voting machines. Such types would include the punch-card and lever voting machines.

Voting Rights for Minorities

What steps were taken to make sure minorities would have fair and equal treatment in future elections in Florida? On January 12, 2001, the U.S. Commission on Civil Rights held hearings on voting problems in the 2000 presidential election. (It is an independent, fact-finding agency founded under the Civil Rights Act of 1957.)

Katherine Harris and Governor Jeb Bush testified at these hearings. They both defended their actions during the 2000 presidential election process. Like Katherine Harris, Jeb Bush had won elective office in Florida in 1998. As the governor of Florida and the top Republican leader in the state, Jeb Bush promised to "deliver" the state to George W. Bush. But his role in helping George W. Bush win the presidency was both professional and personal. Jeb Bush is George's younger brother.

Some Florida voters were also at the hearings to make sure that their voting rights were protected in future elections. They complained of serious problems in the state's election practices. Some African-American voters testified that they were turned away from the polling areas by the presence of police roadblocks. Other voters said that their names were mistakenly removed from voting lists.

Five months later, the commission issued a lengthy report

on its findings. It faulted Governor Jeb Bush and Secretary of State Katherine Harris for not making sure election methods were fair and equal to all voters on Election Day, 2000. What kinds of voting problems did the commission spotlight? It found, for example, that African-American voters cast 54 percent of the votes that were rejected in the state. Yet they represented only 11 percent of the total votes cast. That meant African-American voters were "10 times more likely than white voters to have their ballots rejected."[5] But the commission said it found no real proof that officials purposely tried to exclude minority voters.

Independently of the commission's report, however, Florida lawmakers promised that all voters would receive fair treatment at the polls in the future. For example, registered voters would be allowed to vote even when their names were not on official voting lists.

Where Are They Now?

The 2000 election highlighted key players and losers. The winner, George W. Bush, of course, went on to make news as president of the United States and leader of the free world. But others faded from the flash of TV cameras and reporters because they were no longer newsworthy. Not all the "faded stars" were people. Among them were a troubled agency and a 215-year-old institution. What happened to each and every one of them because of—or, in spite of—their moment in history? Here are some updates on them:

Florida Secretary of State Katherine Harris: She ran for a seat in the U.S. Congress from Florida in 2002, and won. The elective office of secretary of state of Florida, which Harris previously held, ended in January 2003. Florida voters made it an appointed office instead.

Florida Governor Jeb Bush: Was there negative fallout from Florida voters for the way Jeb Bush handled the state's ballot problems in 2000? Only briefly. Jeb Bush ran for reelection in 2002, and won by a landslide.

Former Vice President Al Gore: After his stunning loss in 2000, Gore traveled, taught, lectured, and wrote books. All the while, he was testing his political popularity. In December 2002, Gore announced he would not run for president in the 2004 election. However, he may still have hopes of being president some day. If he ever does become president, Gore would repeat Richard Nixon's route. Nixon lost to John F. Kennedy in 1960, and then skipped the next presidential election. In 1968, Nixon ran and won, defeating the Democratic candidate Hubert Humphrey.

Senator Joseph Lieberman: Remember, he lost his bid for vice president when he and Al Gore were defeated in the 2000 election. But he never gave up his seat in the Senate. At the same time Lieberman was running for vice president, he also ran for reelection to the United States Senate from

Connecticut. Lieberman won the Senate reelection and joined the new Congress.

The Voter News Service: Remember, this agency added up election votes for the television networks. The networks decided to keep the same service despite its poor performance on the night of the election of 2000. The service promised to replace its computer system and software. However, VNS performed poorly in the general election two years later. In fact, VNS was not happy with the results of its own exit polling in the 2002 elections. As a result, it did not release its surveys to news networks. VNS has now disbanded altogether.

The Electoral College: Does the Electoral College still exist? In 2001, there were two unsuccessful proposals in Congress to abolish the Electoral College. But since the birth of the nation, there have been over a thousand constitutional amendments proposed in all.[11]

What would it take to do away with the Electoral College system? Basically, it would require a constitutional amendment. But it is very difficult for any amendment to pass. First, it would take a two-thirds vote in both houses of Congress. Then it would take three-quarters of the fifty states to approve it. Yet, the smaller states would probably not be in favor of doing away with the Electoral College. That is because, given their low populations, they would have much less influence in a presidential election outcome if it were based entirely on popular votes. In the Electoral College system, the smaller states (even though they also have fewer electoral votes than the larger states) can still possibly decide the outcome of an election. So it appears that the Electoral College is here to stay. That is, until another major presidential election crisis brings the issue into the spotlight again.

A New, Divided Congress

Let's not forget that an election is a political event. The 2000 election not only pitted Gore and Bush against each other. It was Democrats against Republicans, too. As a result of the general election, there was a 50-50 split in the Senate. The tie was broken months later when Senator James Jeffords of Vermont left the Republican Party. He continued in office as an Independent. His change of party gained the Democrats a slim lead in the Senate. Republicans still had a slim majority in the House.

Who Really Won in Florida?

Many people wondered what the final vote count in Florida would have been if events had turned out differently? Would Gore have really won? Would Bush have won anyway?

The answer depends on two key factors. One is the type of ballots that were to be recounted. The other is the kind of standards that were to be used to count them. For example,

The 2000 election pitted Democrats against Republicans. But after the decision, there was little bitterness between the parties.

what if the United States Supreme Court and time had allowed the hand recounts of Florida's more than 43,000 rejected undervote ballots to continue in the 2000 election? What if only the undervote ballots in the four Democratic Florida counties were hand counted, as Gore had wanted? What if all the Florida undervotes and overvotes were recounted by hand? It is clear, therefore, that the variety of outcomes would satisfy some people but not everyone.

The confusion over the Florida vote totals was sorted out almost a year after the 2000 presidential election. In one notable study, several large newspapers and other news organizations hired a nonprofit research firm to count by hand the state's nearly 180,000 uncounted ballots.[7] They included The Associated Press, *The New York Times*, CNN, and *The Washington Post*.

First, the examiners established their own specific set of standards for judging ballots with chads. (It was something the Florida lawmakers, Secretary of State Harris, county election officials, and the courts had not done.) Then they made a thorough recount of only the 43,000 ballots originally ordered by the Florida Supreme Court. They found that Bush would *still* have won the Florida vote count by more than 493 votes.[8] That vote total was slightly less than Bush's official lead of 537 popular votes.

The study also found, however, that poorly designed ballots (such as the butterfly ballot) and poorly working voting machines may have cost Gore the election. Remember that thousands of voters had their ballots disqualified when they marked the confusing butterfly ballots twice. Like the courts, the researchers in the study also disqualified these ballots. Why? These experts could not, in good faith, guess a voter's intent in this situation. Which candidate (for example, Al Gore or Pat Buchanan) did a voter actually mean to select when he or she punched two candidates' names on a ballot?

There were more surprising findings. The study suggested that Gore went about his legal campaign in the wrong way. Researchers found that he should have gone to court to make sure that *all* the problem ballots—both undervotes and overvotes in the entire state of Florida—were recounted by hand. Remember that Gore sued in court to have undervote ballots recounted in only four of the state's sixty-seven counties. The study of only the undervote ballots showed that Gore would have picked up several hundred votes in these counties but would have lost in the total vote count in the state anyway. But, if Gore had successfully sued to have *both* overvotes and undervotes recounted in all the counties, they said, his chances of becoming president would have been better. In fact, he may possibly have won by a margin of anywhere from 42 to 171 votes.[9]

How did President George Bush and private citizen Al Gore feel about the results of the study? They both took the news in stride. There were now more important things to worry about. The nation was in the midst of a global war with terrorists.

The September 11 Terrorist Attacks Change Everything

How did the nation change after George W. Bush became president? During his first eight months in office, President George W. Bush centered on domestic policies. Then came the terrorist attacks against the United States. The date was September 11, 2001. That morning Arab terrorists took over four American commercial airliners already in flight. They crashed two of the planes into the Twin Towers of the World Trade Center in New York City. The third plane crashed into the Pentagon building outside Washington, D.C. The fourth plane did not hit its intended mark in the nation's capital. Some passengers managed to overpower the terrorists, and the plane crash-landed in Pennsylvania. The attacks changed the nation almost immediately.

How did President Bush measure up to the challenge of a nation under attack? After all, it was clear that foreign policy was not Bush's strong suit or interest during his campaign for the presidency. After the terrorist attacks, however, President Bush's strong and determined response to the attacks struck the right tones. He received a great amount of support from Americans. There was a spirit of national cooperation and unity, suitable for a nation under attack. The events of September 11 transformed President

After the terrorist attacks that devastated the country on September 11, 2001, President George Bush received strong support for his handling of the crisis situation.

107

Bush into a strong and confident national and world leader. Even former Vice President Al Gore played the role of a loyal citizen who stands behind his president.

What about the news that Bush probably would have won in the recount of Florida's undervote ballots—but not in the recount of both the undervote and overvote ballots? It did not seem to matter now—the nation had already rallied around its new president.

In the End, It's the Votes That Count

By all accounts, the presidential election of 2000 was both the best and the worst of times for Americans. In the end, it was not just about who won or lost. The story was more than the sum of all its players. The players included not only the candidates. They were also the electoral system and Florida's flawed election law. Then, too, they were the legal battles, the lower courts, and the United States Supreme Court's decision in the *Bush* v. *Gore* case.

Clearly, some of the benefits of the 2000 election were the unique learning opportunities. The entire experience served as a model wake-up call for all Americans. It reminded them that they needed to learn about how their government works. They needed to get involved in its different processes. How can people become active at the local, state, and national levels? They can take an active part in political parties, campaigns, and elections. (Underage voters can take part in school elections.) Perhaps most important is the act of voting, if only to make government leaders answerable and responsible for their actions.

For many Americans, voting is a time-honored tradition. It is a right that they fought hard to get or to keep. Yet, sadly, other Americans of voting age today do not bother to vote in a local or state elections, or even a presidential election. Voter turnout for presidential elections dropped 25 percent in the last forty years.[10]

People give many reasons for not voting. Some argue that their votes do not really matter in the final outcome of an election. The extremely close 2000 presidential election

The presidential election of 2000 proved to many people the importance of voting.

race between Bush and Gore proved them wrong. Only about 51 percent of eligible Americans voted in that election.[11] That is a total of about 105 million voters. Yet, in the end, only several hundred votes in only one state in the nation determined the winner.

The story does not really end here. Will voters in future presidential elections show up in greater or fewer numbers than the 2000 election? The answer will underscore voter confidence in the election process—or the lack of it. And that will be one important legacy of *Bush* v. *Gore.*

Questions for Discussion

1. Did the Florida Supreme Court overstep its bounds by ruling that hand recounting of ballots should continue?

2. Are hand recounts of ballots more accurate than machine counts?

3. Did the United States Supreme Court overstep its bounds by ruling that the recounting of Florida ballots should stop?

4. Is the reputation of the United States Supreme Court damaged because it involved itself in the presidential election of 2000?

5. Did the Supreme Court set a dangerous precedent for future presidential elections by deciding the 2000 presidential election?

6. In the wake of the United States Supreme Court decision in *Bush* v. *Gore*, will fewer people bother to vote for president the next time?

7. How would you get more people to vote in presidential elections?

8. Should either Al Gore or George W. Bush have quit the presidential race without challenging the Florida vote counts in the courts? Was either candidate a sore loser?

9. Do you believe George W. Bush won the presidency fair and square? Why or why not?

10. Should the Electoral College be replaced by a direct popular election of a president?

11. What are some advantages and disadvantages to the Electoral College system?

12. Should polling places across the country close at the same time?

13. How would you improve the election process and the voting system?

14. Should news networks wait until the polls close in a state before predicting the outcome of an election?

Chapter Notes

Chapter 1. Building a Case

1. Tom Raum, "President-Elect Bush Seeks Unity," © *The Associated Press*, <http://www.americaonline.com> (December 19, 2000).

2. "A Night to Remember, Part I," *Time* Special Edition, Winter 2000-2001, p. 24. [no author given]

3. Kirsten Danis, "When Veep Retracted, W. Acted by Hanging Up," *New York Post*, December 6, 2000, p. 5.

4. "Election 2000: A Special Report," *Newsday*, December 14, 2000, p. 5. [no author given]

5. *Bush* v. *Gore*, 531 U.S. ___ (2000).

6. "Jeffrey Toobin: Election 2000 Anniversary," November 7, 2001, CNN.com, © 2001 Cable News Network, (November 11, 2001).

7. Touchston v. McDermott, 2000 WL 1781942, *6 & n. 19 (CA11) (Tjoflat, J., dissenting) <http://www.law.com> © 2001 Law. Com, (May, 21, 2001) (see p. 10 of decision).

Chapter 2. Election of the President

1. Professor Howard Gillman, "The Role of Courts, Law and Politics in Election 2000," December 13, 2001, <http://www.usc.edu> (December, 14, 2001).

2. *Bush* v. *Gore*, 531 U.S. ___ (2000).

3. *Jones* v. *Bush*, 00-953.

Chapter 3. The Road to the Supreme Court

1. Marilyn Rauber, "Papa George Joins Son on 'Roller Coaster,'" *New York Post*, November 30, 2000, p. 7.

2. *Siegel* v. *LePore*, 120 F.Supp.2d 1041.

3. *Palm Beach County Canvassing Board* v. *Harris*, 772 So.2d 1220.

4. *Bush* v. *Palm Beach County Canvassing Board*, 531 U.S. 70, 121 S.Ct. 471.

5. Ibid.

6. *Jacobs* v. *Seminole County Canvassing Board*, 2000 WL 1793429.

7. *Taylor* v. *Martin County Canvassing Board*, 2000 WL 1793409.

8. Linda McKenney, "By the Numbers," *Newsday*, December 14, 2000, p. 2.

9. *Gore* v. *Harris*, 456 So. 2d 1314 (Fla. 3d DC).

10. *Gore* v. *Harris*, 772 So.2d 1243 (Fla.2000).

11. Michael Kramer, "W.'s Recount Fallback Plan," *Daily News*, November 22, 2000, p. 5.

12. Richard Morin and Claudia Deane, "Poll Finds Most Want Recount as Last Word," *Washington Post*, November 14, 2000, p. A20.

13. Deborah Orin, "Q & A on the Florida Fiasco's Latest Developments," *New York Post*, November 30, 2000, p. 4.

14. Deborah Orin, "Throw in the Towel or Be Hung Out to Dry," *New York Post*, December 5, 2000, p. 3.

15. Marilyn Rauber, "Al Insists He's Still Optimistic," *New York Post*, December 6, 2000, p. 5.

16. Brian Blomquist, "Gore Takes His Case to the People," *New York Post*, November 28, 2000, p. 2.

17. William Glaberson, "Florida Justices May Have Put Cart First, Experts Say," *The New York Times*, December 10, 2000, p. 44.

18. Dexter Filkins and Dana Canedy, "U.S. Supreme Court's Ruling Stops Florida's Election Workers in Their Tracks," *The New York Times*, December 10, 2000, p. 43.

19. "Scalia and Stevens Clash Over Recount Stay in *Bush v. Gore*," December 10, 2000 CNN.com, law center (September 2, 2001). [no author given]

Chapter 4. The Case for George W. Bush

1. Tony Mauro, "Justices Kennedy, Thomas Discuss 'Bush v. Gore,' Minority Law Clerks at 11th Circuit Conference," *American Lawyers Media*, May 21, 2001, <http://www.law.com> (May 21, 2001).

2. "Election Hearing Concludes at U.S. Supreme Court," © 2000 *The Associated Press*, December 11, 2000, <http://www.americaonline> (December 11, 2000).

3. Garrett Therolf, "Crowds Protest Outside Supreme Court," © 2000 *The Associated Press*, December 11, 2000, <http://www.americaonline> (December 11, 2000).

4. "U.S. Supreme Court Arguments," <http://www.washingtonpost.com> (March 11, 2002).

5. Tony Mauro, "Justices Kennedy, Thomas Discuss 'Bush v. Gore,' Minority Law Clerks at 11th Circuit Conference," American Lawyers Media, May 21, 2001, <http://www.law.com> (May 21, 2001).

6. Brief of Petitioner, *Bush* v. *Gore*, 531 U.S. ___ (2000). (No. 00–949).

7. *Bush* v. *Gore*, 531 U.S. ___ (2000).

8. Brief of Petitioner, *Bush* v. *Gore*, 531 U.S. ___ (2000). (No. 00-949).

9. *Bush* v. *Gore*, 531 U.S. ___ (2000).

10. Bo Li, "*Bush* v. *Gore* and the Relationship Between Rule of Law and Democracy," *Perspectives*, vol. 2, No. 3, <http://www.oycf.org> (March 8, 2002).

11. Brief of Petitioner, *Bush* v. *Gore*, 531 U.S. ___ (2000). (No. 00–949).

12. Ibid.

13. *Bush* v. *Gore*, 531 U.S. ___ (2000).

14. Brief of Petitioner, *Bush* v. *Gore*, 531 U.S. ___ (2000). (No. 00–949).

15. Ibid.

Chapter 5. The Case for Al Gore

1. *Bush* v. *Gore*, 531 U.S. ___ (2000).

2. Brief of Respondent, *Bush* v. *Gore*, 531 U.S. ___ (2000). (No. 00–949).

3. *Bush* v. *Gore*, 531 U.S. ___ (2000).

4. Ibid.

5. Ibid.

6. "U.S. Supreme Court Arguments," <http://www.washingtonpost.com> (March 11, 2002).

7. *Bush* v. *Gore*, 531 U.S. ___ (2000).

8. Brief of Respondent, *Bush* v. *Gore*, 531 U.S. ___ (2000). (No. 00-949).

Chapter 6. The Decision

1. *Bush* v. *Gore*, 531 U.S. ___ (2000).

2. Ibid.

3. Ibid.

4. Ibid.

5. *Bush* v. *Gore*, 531 U.S. ___ , Ginsburg, J., dissenting opinion, (2000).

6. *Bush* v. *Gore*, 531 U.S. ___ (2000).

7. *Bush* v. *Gore*, 531 U.S. ___ , Ginsburg, J., dissenting opinion, (2000).

8. Dr. Reginald Shareef, "Politics, Ambition, and the Decision in *Bush v. Gore*," December 18, 2000, <http://www.roanoke.com/magazine> (March 8, 2002).

9. "How Kennedy Won Hawaii," Joshua Leinsdorf, Institute of Election Analysis, <http://www.leinsdorf.com> (March 21, 2002).

10. Jessica Kowal, "Gore's Worst Enemy: Time," *Newsday*, December 14, 2000, p. 20.

11. Reuters, Washington, "Vice President Al Gore's Concession Speech," December 13, 2000, © 2000 Reuters Limited, <http://www.aol.com> (December 14, 2000).

12. Ibid.

13. Reuters, Washington, "Vice President Al Gore's Concession Speech," December 13, 2000, © 2000 Reuters Limited, <http://www.aol.com> (December 14, 2000).

14. Ibid.

15. Reuters, Washington, "Text of George W. Bush's Speech," December 13, 2000, © 2000 Reuters Limited, <http:// www.aol.com> (December 14, 2000).

16. Deborah Orin, "Q & A on the Florida Fiasco's Latest Developments," *New York Post*, November 30, 2000, p. 4.

17. Anne Gearan, "High Court Ruling May Taint Court" © The Associated Press, December 13, 2000, <http://www.aol.com> (December 13, 2000).

18. Hugo Kugiya, "Point of View of the People," *Newsday*, December 14, 2000, p. 19.

19. Andy Greene, "To the Editor," December 11, 2000, *The New York Times*, OP Ed Letters, "A Teacher's Lesson," December 13, 2000, <http://www.nytimes> (December 13, 2000).

20. Hugo Kugiya, "Point of View of the People," *Newsday*, December 14, 2000, p. 19.

Chapter 7. Where Do We Stand Today?

1. *Bush* v. *Gore*, 531 U.S. ___ (2000).

2. Ibid.

3. "Dell Plans Electronic Voting System," by The Associated Press, *The New York Times*, June 4, 2001, <http://www. nytimes.com> (June 4, 2001).

4. B. J. Palermo, "'*Bush v. Gore*' Lives On," *The National Law Journal*, September 10, 2001, <http://www.law.com> (March 21, 2002).

5. "Civil Rights Commission Says Florida Election Unfair to Blacks," <http://CNN.com> June 5, 2001, © 2001 *The Associated Press* (June 5, 2001).

6. "Numbers," *Time*, November 27, 2001, p. 27.

7. "Florida Recount Study: Bush Still Wins," *CNN.com In-Depth Specials*, © 2002 Cable News Network, <http:// www.10.cc.com > (November 12, 2002).

8. Ibid.

9. "Florida Vote Review: Gore's Legal Strategy Ensured Bush Win," November 12, 2001, <http://www.foxnews.com> (November 12, 2001).

10. Michael Rust, "One for the History Books," December 4, 2000, *Insight on the News*, <http://www.find-articles.com> (June 28, 2001).

11. "Final Tabulation Shows Almost 105.4 Million Voters," December 19, 2000, <http://www.cnn.com> (December 19, 2000).

Glossary

appeal—A request by one of the parties in a lawsuit to have a higher court review a lower court's ruling on a case.

appeals court—A court that reviews a lower court's ruling on a case at the request of one of the parties in a lawsuit.

brief—A written argument in a legal case. It is filed by a lawyer to the judge or Justice in a case.

concur—To agree with the conclusions or results of another Justice's opinion filed in a case. However, the Justice in agreement may not necessarily have the same reasons.

defendant—In a civil (not criminal) lawsuit, it is the person who is sued. In a criminal case, it is the person who is accused of a crime.

dissent—To disagree with the conclusions or results of another Justice's opinion filed in a case.

Due Process Clause—This clause is in Section 1 of the Fourteenth Amendment to the Constitution. It is the right to have laws applied fairly to all persons. It applies to state government and state courts.

Equal Protection Clause—This clause is in Section 1 of the Fourteenth Amendment to the Constitution. It is the right to equal protection of laws. (It was originally passed to guarantee equal protection to freed black slaves.)

federal law—A law that is created and passed by the United States Congress.

Fourteenth Amendment—Section 1 guarantees the rights to "due process" and "equal protection."

lawsuit—A legal action between two parties in a court of law.

oral arguments—Arguments made by lawyers for their clients on the issues of a case before the Justices of the United States Supreme Court.

per curiam ("by the court")—A written but unsigned decision in which the Supreme Court speaks with one voice rather than by a single Justice.

petitioner—A person who begins a court proceeding.

plaintiff—The party who is suing someone else in a civil lawsuit.

remand—To send back. An appeals court may, as part of its decision, send a case back to a lower court for further action.

respondent—The defendant at the Supreme Court level.

stay order—An order by a court to stop an action until further proceedings are taken.

writ of certiorari—An order by an appeals court to hear the appeal of a case from a lower court. Also, the United States Supreme Court, at its choosing, may grant a petition to review a case.

Further Reading

Dershowitz, Alan M. *Supreme Injustice: How the High Court Hijacked Election 2000.* New York: Oxford University Press, 2001.

Ellis, Joseph J. *Founding Brothers: The Revolutionary Generation.* New York: Vintage Books, 2002.

Greenfield, Jeff. *"Oh, Waiter! One Order of Crow!": Inside the Strangest Presidential Election Finish in American History.* New York: Penguin USA, 2001.

Kaplan, David A. *The Accidental President: How 413 Lawyers, 9 Supreme Court Justices, and 5,963,110 (Give or Take a Few) Floridians Landed George W. Bush in the White House.* New York: William Morrow & Co., 2001.

Posner, Richard A. *Breaking the Deadlock: The 2000 Election, the Constitution, and the Courts.* Princeton: Princeton University Press, 2001.

Raskin, Jamin B. *We the Students: Supreme Court Cases for and about Students.* Washington, D.C.: CQ Press, 2000.

Rehnquist, William H. *Supreme Court: A New Edition of the Chief Justice's Classic History.* New York: Knopf, 2001.

Ryan Jr., Bernard. *Community Service for Teens/Participating in Government,* Vol. 5. Chicago: Ferguson Publishing, 1998.

Schlesinger, Arthur Meier, Fred L. Israel, Jonathon H. Mann, eds. *The Election of 2000 and the Administration of George W. Bush.* Broomall, Penn.: Mason Crest Publishers, 2003.

Internet Addresses

InfoPlease.com: The Supreme Court

Get the facts about the Supreme Court Justices, the history of their decisions, milestone cases, and more.

<http://www.infoplease.com/ipa/A0873869.html>

TeenGov

Find out about the political powers citizens have in the United States. Includes facts about the Supreme Court, state governments, Congress, and the president.

<http://www.teengov.org>

Index

124

126